The Women's Institute

theWI
INSPIRING WOMEN

chocolate
success

SIMON &
SCHUSTER
ILLUSTRATED

London · New York · Sydney · Toronto
A CBS COMPANY

Sara Lewis

First published in Great Britain
by Simon & Schuster UK Ltd, 2011
A CBS Company

Simon & Schuster
Illustrated Books,
Simon & Schuster UK Ltd, 1st Floor,
222 Gray's Inn Road, London WC1X 8HB

1 2 3 4 5 6 7 8 9 10

Senior Commissioning Editor: **Nicky Hill**
Project Editor: **Nicki Lampon**
Designer: **Fiona Andreanelli**
Food Photographer: **William Shaw**
Stylist: **Tony Hutchinson**
Home Economist: **Sara Lewis**

Colour reproduction by Dot Gradations Ltd, UK
Printed and bound in China

A CIP catalogue for this book is available from the
British Library.

ISBN 978-0-85720-258-1

In memory of Michael Shaw

Contents

Introduction

There are very few of us who can resist a slice of chocolate cake, a gooey chocolate pudding or a scoop of good chocolate ice cream – not forgetting a square or two of chocolate.

Since its first mention in history, chocolate has been described as an aphrodisiac. Legend has it that the Aztec Emperor Montezuma supposedly drank 50 cups of hot chocolate a day before visiting his harem. King Charles II was convinced that hot chocolate was an aphrodisiac, as were his contemporaries in Europe. Even Casanova abandoned champagne in favour of chocolate! While a box of chocolates is still the most celebrated gift for Valentine's Day.

Chocolate is one of the best natural sources of arginine, an amino acid that acts in a similar way to Viagra. Many women are sometimes unkindly teased that they prefer chocolate to sex. While this may be a little unfair, eating chocolate does bring pleasure and a feeling of well being. This can be attributed to the fact that it triggers mood enhancing substances in the body, almost making it nature's alternative to Prozac! Perhaps less well known is the fact that chocolate also contains natural stimulants such as caffeine, which increase alertness. Surprisingly, a 125 g (4½ oz) bar of dark chocolate contains more caffeine than a cup of instant coffee.

This book contains recipes to tempt and celebrate every occasion. From an accompaniment with coffee to a delicious dessert, from a birthday celebration to those moments when you really long for a dessert but don't have much time, there's something for everyone.

Devil's food cake, page 89

Notes on the recipes

- Both metric and imperial measurements have been given in all recipes. Use one set of measurements only and not a mixture of both. Spoon measures are level and 1 tablespoon = 15 ml, 1 teaspoon = 5 ml.

- Preheat ovens before use and cook on the centre shelf unless cooking more than one item. If using a fan oven, reduce the heat by 10–20°C, but check with your handbook. Ovens vary considerably, so get to know your own and adjust accordingly. Check cakes by opening the door a fraction, and turn tins if cakes seem to be browning on one side. Look at cakes 5–10 minutes before the end of cooking and test if needs be. If not quite done by the end of the cooking time, cook a little longer.

- Medium eggs have been used. This book contains some recipes made with raw or lightly cooked eggs. Pregnant or breast-feeding women, invalids, the elderly and very young children should avoid these dishes. Once prepared, keep refrigerated.

- This book also contains recipes made with nuts. Those with known allergic reactions to nuts and nut derivatives, pregnant and breast-feeding women and very young children should avoid these dishes.

Types of chocolate

Rather like wine, we are now beginning to be more aware of where our chocolate comes from. The majority comes from Africa between the Ivory Coast and Ghana, but the very best comes from Ecuador and Venezuela in South America, Madagascar in Africa and the Dominican Republic in the Caribbean. Like grapes, the flavours of chocolate vary depending on its country of origin, the soil and climate and differences in the fermentation process. The quality of the cocoa beans will also affect the flavour, along with the percentage of cocoa solids in the chocolate.

Dark chocolate – a luxurious, strong-flavoured chocolate will contain 70–75% cocoa solids and just a small amount of sugar. Also available is chocolate containing 85% cocoa solids, but this produces a very strong, almost bitter flavour.

Milk chocolate – a creamy, delicately flavoured chocolate as the name suggests. It can contain 35–40% cocoa solids, so will vary in colour – the more cocoa solids it has, the darker and stronger the colour. Try Ecuadorian milk chocolate as a good halfway point. It is darker in colour than a true milk chocolate and delicious mixed with honey, spices or nuts. Avoid milk chocolate that has other fats added.

White chocolate – some argue that this is not a true chocolate as it does not contain any cocoa solids at all. Made with cocoa butter, sugar, milk and sometimes vanilla, it must be melted carefully; overheating causes it to 'seize' into a firm lump, spoiling the texture. It varies considerably in quality – choose brands that contain cocoa butter and no additional animal or vegetable fat as this will give an inferior flavour and greasy aftertaste.

Couverture chocolate – used mainly by professional chocolatiers. Available in dark, milk and white chocolate from specialist cake decorating and catering suppliers. Generally sold as buttons or oval discs for quick and easy melting, it has a high proportion of cocoa solids and only naturally occurring fat. Valrhona is thought to be the best with 64% cocoa content. Most often sold untempered, so check before using.

Cocoa powder – this is made by removing nearly all the cocoa butter from the chocolate liquor using a press. The remaining cocoa solids are then ground, sifted and mixed with potassium carbonate to make the powder soluble in water (or milk). Depending on the brand, it may also be sweetened.

Melting chocolate

For the best results, melt chocolate over water in a bain marie. Pour about 4 cm (1½ inches) of water into a saucepan, heat until barely simmering then place a bowl over the top of the pan. Make sure it stands proud of the pan so no moisture will be able to get into the chocolate and spoil the finish. So that the chocolate does not overheat, or 'seize' into a solid grainy lump, make sure that the water does not touch the base of the bowl. Vary the size of the pan depending on the quantity of chocolate that you are melting.

Chocolate can also be melted in the microwave but this is suitable for small quantities only. Microwave in 30 second bursts on full power or a medium setting depending on the wattage of your machine. Allow 30–60 seconds standing time between bursts to allow the heat to equalise. White chocolate has a higher milk and sugar content so burns easily, especially where hot spots occur. Take great care and only melt very small amounts at a time on a medium setting.

Using moulds

Silicone moulds are available in a variety of shapes. When making solid shapes, pipe or spoon melted chocolate into them then tap the mould to release any air bubbles. For hollow shapes, cover with a thick layer of melted chocolate, turn the mould upside down to allow excess chocolate to drain back into the pan then leave to set turned up the right way. For larger shapes it can be a good idea to recoat the mould thinly several times. Once set, the chocolate will contract slightly and as the mould is flexed gently the chocolate shape should come out easily. Always use tempered chocolate when using moulds.

Make sure you keep moulds scrupulously clean. Wash thoroughly with detergent, rinse then dry using a soft, lint-free cloth or soft tissue. Avoid touching the inside of the moulds as this can cause blemishes or the chocolate to stick. When removing the set chocolate remains don't use metal knives or spoons as these can damage the moulds, use a plastic spatula instead or soak in warm water to remove any last remnants of chocolate.

Techniques

Chocolate caraque – Like so many things, there is a knack to this and the key is the angle at which you hold the knife. Begin by spreading melted chocolate over a marble board until about 5 mm (¼ inch) thick. Leave in a cool place to set (not the fridge) then, using a large cook's knife and holding the tip with one hand and the handle with the other, cut with a slight see-saw action with the knife at a 45° angle across the chocolate until long curls have been made. Alternatively, larger, more open curls can be made in the same way with a new wallpaper scraper. For two-tone caraque, pipe or spoon thick alternate lines of dark and white chocolate over a marble board, lightly spread with a palette knife to smooth the top surface then leave to cool and set. Draw the knife over the top as above.

Cheat's curls – If you don't have much time, curls can be made using a swivel-bladed vegetable peeler. The secret is to soften unwrapped chocolate slightly in the microwave. Allow 20 seconds on full power for a 200 g (7 oz) bar then place the bar with the flat side uppermost and the long edge resting against the edge of a chopping board or work surface. Run the vegetable peeler along the long side. The curls will grow in size the more you do. If they are very thin, warm the chocolate once more in the microwave and then try again. Store in a paper-lined plastic box in a cool place or the fridge.

Piped decorations – Half-fill a paper piping bag with melted chocolate, fold the top over several times so that the chocolate cannot escape then, if necessary, snip a tiny bit from the tip. There is no need to add a piping nozzle unless you have one. Pipe small decorative shapes on to a baking sheet lined with non-stick baking paper.

Chocolate scribbles – Pipe random scribbles over a baking sheet lined with non-stick baking paper. Chill until firm then pipe a second layer in a different coloured melted chocolate. Chill, then ease the chocolate off the paper, break into shards and arrange at angles on the top of a cream-covered cake or mousse.

Using acetate/non-stick baking paper – Melted chocolate makes an effective wrapping for a more formal cake. Buy sheets of acetate from good stationers, or use non-stick baking paper to make a strip the circumference and height of your cake. Spread just-melted chocolate over the acetate or paper then wrap around the cake so that the chocolate is touching the side of the cake and the acetate or paper is on the outside. Trim the ends if needed. They must butt together – if they overlap you will find it very difficult to remove the acetate or paper when the chocolate has set. Chill until the chocolate is firm then peel away the acetate or paper (see

Chocolate flower basket, page 93 and Chocolate truffle cake, page 98).

Chocolate leaves – This easy decoration is made by painting just-melted chocolate over the underside of some clean rose or mint leaves. Leave a little space at the top of the leaf so that when the chocolate is set you have something to hold as you peel the leaf from the chocolate. Holly or bay leaves may also be covered, but these are best painted on their top shiny surface.

Dipped decorations – A selection of fruits half dipped into melted dark, milk or white chocolate can make an effective and easy decoration to finish off a special cake (see Black Forest roulade, page 80), mousse or brulée, or serve with a scoop of homemade ice cream or sorbet. Choose from fresh cherries, still on their stalks, strawberries still with their green tops in place or cape gooseberries (physallis) with their papery casing torn into four and then peeled away from the fruit and twisted attractively. When making petits fours, half dip pecan nuts or walnuts sandwiched together with a little homemade marzipan.

Quick and easy bakes

Chocolate cup cakes

Extremely fashionable at the moment, these upmarket-looking chocolate cup cakes are decorated with a piped chocolate and mascarpone frosting.

Makes 12
Preparation time:
  30 minutes +
  30–45 minutes chilling +
  cooling
Cooking time: 15 minutes

25 g (1 oz) cocoa powder
3 tablespoons boiling water
3 eggs
175 g (6 oz) light muscovado
  sugar
175 g (6 oz) soft margarine or
  butter, at room temperature
175 g (6 oz) self-raising flour

Chocolate frosting
75 g (2¾ oz) dark chocolate
  (70% cocoa), broken into pieces
250 g (9 oz) mascarpone cheese
50 g (1¾ oz) icing sugar (no need
  to sift)
1 teaspoon vanilla essence

Preheat the oven to 180°C/350°F/Gas Mark 4. Line 12 sections of a muffin tin with 3 cm (1¼ inch) deep foil cup cake cases.

Mix the cocoa powder with the boiling water in a small bowl until smooth. Place the eggs, sugar, margarine or butter and flour in a large bowl, add the cocoa paste and beat with a wooden spoon or electric mixer until smooth.

Divide the mixture between the cases and smooth the surface of each. Bake for 15 minutes until well risen, lightly domed and the tops spring back when lightly pressed with a fingertip. Leave to cool.

Meanwhile, melt the chocolate for the frosting in a bowl set over a saucepan of gently simmering water. Take off the heat and leave to cool slightly.

Beat the mascarpone cheese, icing sugar and vanilla essence together until just mixed. Gradually whisk the cheese mixture into the chocolate, one-quarter at a time, mixing until smooth before adding the next portion. Chill in the fridge for 30–45 minutes until thick enough to pipe or spread.

Spoon the frosting into a piping bag fitted with a medium star nozzle and pipe over the top of the cakes. If you don't have a piping bag, spread with a round bladed knife. Keep in a cool place until required.

Tip These are best eaten on the day they are made but any remaining cakes can be stored in a plastic box in the fridge. They can also be frozen – decorate, open freeze until firm then transfer to a plastic box. Freeze for up to 6 weeks and defrost, uncovered, at room temperature for 1½–2 hours before serving.

Chocolate drop scones

Make these with Ecuadorian milk chocolate – it is the colour of dark chocolate but has a creamy, milder taste.

Serves 4
Preparation time:
  20 minutes
Cooking time: 15 minutes

175 g (6 oz) **plain flour**
1 teaspoon **baking powder**
½ teaspoons **bicarbonate of soda**
25 g (1 oz) **icing sugar**
2 **eggs**, separated
150 g (5½ oz) **low fat natural yogurt**
150 ml (5 fl oz) **semi-skimmed milk**
100 g (3½ oz) **milk chocolate (39% cocoa)**, diced
sunflower oil

Maple and chocolate sauce
8 tablespoons **maple syrup**
100 g (3½ oz) **milk chocolate (39% cocoa)**

To serve
2 ripe **peaches**, stoned and sliced, to serve
vanilla ice cream (optional)

Sift the flour, baking powder, bicarbonate of soda and icing sugar into a large bowl. In a separate bowl, whisk the egg whites until they form soft, moist-looking peaks. Add the egg yolks and yogurt to the flour mixture then gradually whisk in the milk until the mixture is thick and smooth. Fold in the diced chocolate then the egg whites.

Heat a large, non-stick frying pan or flat griddle and rub with a piece of folded kitchen towel drizzled with a little sunflower oil. Drop spoonfuls of the batter on to the pan, leaving space between each for them to rise, and cook over a medium heat until the underside is golden and the tops are bubbly. Turn over and cook the second side until golden and the centre is cooked through.

While the drop scones cook, place the maple syrup and chocolate in a small saucepan and cook over a very gentle heat, stirring occasionally until the chocolate has melted.

When the first batch of drop scones are ready, lift out of the pan and keep warm between sheets of non-stick baking paper inside a clean folded tea towel. Grease the pan again and continue until all the batter has been used up.

Arrange the drop scones on serving plates, allowing three or four per portion depending on your appetite, top with sliced peaches and drizzle with the sauce. Add a scoop of vanilla ice cream, if liked.

Tips Instead of natural yogurt and milk, try using a 284 ml carton of buttermilk. Although ordinary milk will work, the acidity in the yogurt or buttermilk works with the raising agent to make the drop scones rise that extra bit.

If you don't think you will eat all the pancakes in one sitting, then slightly undercook the ones you don't think you will have room for and reheat in a hot, greased pan later in the day.

Triple chocolate cookies

These are almost worth making just for the wonderful smell during baking. Soft, gooey and just packed with chocolate, they will be an instant hit.

Makes about 20
Preparation time:
  20 minutes + cooling
Cooking time:
  10–12 minutes

225 g (8 oz) plain flour
40 g (1½ oz) cocoa powder (no need to sift)
½ teaspoon bicarbonate of soda
150 g (5½ oz) caster sugar
100 g (3½ oz) light muscovado sugar
2 eggs, beaten
175 g (6 oz) butter, melted, plus extra for greasing
1 teaspoon vanilla essence
250 g (9 oz) mixed white, dark and milk chocolate, diced

Preheat the oven to 180°C/350°F/Gas Mark 4.

Place the flour, cocoa powder and bicarbonate of soda in a large bowl, add both sugars and fork together.

Add the eggs, melted butter and vanilla essence and roughly mix with a fork. Add the chocolate pieces and mix until well combined.

Using a small ice cream scoop or two spoons, scoop the mixture into mounds on two greased baking sheets, leaving space between them to spread during baking.

Bake for 10–12 minutes until the tops are cracked and the biscuits are a little darker but still soft. Leave to cool for a few minutes on the baking sheets to harden slightly then transfer to a wire rack to cool completely.

Tips For younger children, or adults who prefer milk chocolate, leave out the cocoa powder and add 40 g (1½ oz) of extra plain flour. Use 250 g (9 oz) of mixed milk and white diced chocolate.

For serious chocoholics, drizzle with random lines of melted white chocolate once the cookies have cooled.

Chequerboard biscuits

These eye-catching biscuits are made by alternating layers of orange and chocolate shortbread dough for a striking Battenburg cake effect.

Makes 20
Preparation time:
 30 minutes + 30 minutes
 chilling + cooling
Cooking time:
 12–15 minutes

2 tablespoons cocoa powder
4 teaspoons boiling water
225 g (8 oz) plain flour
25 g (1 oz) cornflour
175 g (6 oz) butter, cut into pieces
75 g (2¾ oz) caster sugar
grated zest of ½ an orange

Mix the cocoa powder and boiling water in a small bowl until it forms a thick paste. Set aside.

Put the flour, cornflour, butter and sugar in a bowl and rub in the butter with your fingertips or an electric mixer until the mixture looks like fine crumbs. Scoop out half the mixture (250 g/9 oz) into a separate bowl.

Add the orange zest to the first bowl, mix together then squeeze the crumbs to make a soft dough. Add the cocoa paste to the second bowl, mix together then squeeze as before to make a smooth dough.

Roll out the orange shortbread on a piece of non-stick baking paper, pressing with your fingertips to neaten the corners and make a 23 x 18 cm (9 x 7 inch) rectangle. Do the same with the chocolate shortbread on a second sheet of paper. Lift the chocolate shortbread on to the orange shortbread, peeling off the paper as you go.

Cut the stacked shortbread into three 18 cm (7 inch) long strips. Cut the first strip into four narrow 18 cm (7 inch) long strips and turn over the second and fourth strip so that the orange layer is uppermost. Push these strips together to make one strip with alternating colours in both layers.

Cut the second strip as the first one, turning the first and third narrow strips, and place these strips on top of the first four in a Battenburg pattern. You should have alternating colours in all layers. Repeat with the final strip turning the second and fourth narrow strips, to create a six-strip high biscuit that is four strips wide. Chill for 30 minutes.

Preheat the oven to 160°C/325°F/Gas Mark 3.

Cut the biscuit stack into thin slices and arrange on an ungreased baking sheet. Bake for 12–15 minutes until very lightly browned. Leave to cool on the baking sheet then transfer to a plate or biscuit tin.

Tip Rather than cut the two layered shortbread into strips, it can be rolled up and then sliced for a spiral pattern instead.

Cut 'n' come again cookies

Make up a batch of these chunky cookies and keep in the fridge. Just slice off and bake when you need them for that irresistible fresh-baked aroma.

Makes about 20
Preparation time:
25 minutes + cooling
Cooking time: 15 minutes

250 g (9 oz) plain flour
100 g (3½ oz) light muscovado
    sugar
a pinch of salt
1 teaspoon ground cinnamon
175 g (6 oz) butter, diced, plus
    extra for greasing
75 g (2¾ oz) dark chocolate
    (70% cocoa), diced
75 g (2¾ oz) milk chocolate
    (32% cocoa), diced
50 g (1¾ oz) hazelnuts, very
    roughly chopped

Put the flour, sugar, salt and cinnamon into a bowl and mix together. Add the butter then rub in with your fingertips or an electric mixer until the mixture resembles fine crumbs. Continue mixing until the crumbs begin to stick together then squeeze with your hands until you have a rough ball.

Turn the mixture out on to a work surface (there is no need to flour first) and knead in the dark and milk chocolate and nuts.

Put on a large sheet of foil and form a 30 cm (12 inch) sausage shape with a diameter of about 5 cm (2 inches). Roll back and forth into a smooth shape. Wrap in the foil and store in the fridge until needed or for up to 3 days.

When ready to cook, preheat the oven to 180°C/350°F/ Gas Mark 4. Unwrap the biscuit dough and cut into slices about 1 cm (½ inch) thick. Transfer to greased baking sheets and bake for 15 minutes until lightly browned. Loosen the biscuits from the tray and transfer to a wire rack to cool, or serve while still slightly warm if preferred.

Tips After slicing, rewrap any remaining biscuit dough and return it to the fridge.

Experiment with flavour combinations of your own. Try 1 teaspoon of vanilla essence instead of the cinnamon, or a little finely grated orange zest. Or add some chopped dates or a little chopped glacé ginger instead of the nuts.

Raspberry choc muffins

These light, fluffy muffins are best eaten while still warm from the oven. Delicious for a special weekend brunch or for relaxing with a coffee.

Makes 12
Preparation time:
  20 minutes + cooling
Cooking time: 20 minutes

175 g (6 oz) caster sugar
125 ml (4 fl oz) sunflower oil
1 teaspoon vanilla essence
3 eggs
250 ml (9 fl oz) full fat crème
  fraîche
300 g (10½ oz) plain flour
2 teaspoons baking powder
175 g (6 oz) fresh raspberries
150 g (5½ oz) white chocolate,
  diced

Preheat the oven to 200°C/400°F/Gas Mark 6 and line a 12 hole muffin tin with paper cases or squares of non-stick baking paper.

Put the sugar, oil, vanilla essence and eggs into a large bowl and whisk together until just mixed. Add the crème fraîche and mix briefly until just smooth.

Sift in the flour and baking powder then stir together. Fold in two-thirds of the raspberries and chocolate then spoon the mixture into the paper cases. Press the remaining raspberries into the tops and sprinkle with the remaining chocolate.

Bake for about 20 minutes until the muffins are well risen, golden brown and the tops spring back when lightly pressed with a fingertip. Leave to cool for 5 minutes then lift out of the tin and transfer to a wire rack. Serve while still slightly warm.

Tip Try with blueberries or a mix of blueberries and raspberries, or use 150 g (5½ oz) of diced, ready-to-eat dried apricots instead of fresh fruit.

Gooey nut brownies

Soft, gooey, dark chocolate squares. The secret to a really good brownie is in the cooking, so keep an eye on them towards the end of the cooking time.

Cuts into 24 squares
Preparation time:
 30 minutes + cooling
Cooking time:
 20–25 minutes

250 g (9 oz) dark chocolate
 (70% cocoa), broken into pieces
250 g (9 oz) butter, diced
100 g (3½ oz) hazelnuts
4 eggs
250 g (9 oz) caster sugar
1 teaspoon vanilla essence
100 g (3½ oz) self-raising flour
1 teaspoon baking powder

Chocolate topping
75 g (2¾ oz) dark chocolate
 (70% cocoa), melted

Preheat the oven to 180°C/350°F/Gas Mark 4. Line a roasting tin with a base measurement of 18 x 28 cm (7 x 11 inches) with a large piece of non-stick baking paper and snip into the corners diagonally so that when the paper is pressed into the tin it lines the base and sides.

Put the chocolate and butter into a bowl and set over a saucepan of gently simmering water. Leave until melted.

Meanwhile, dry fry the hazelnuts, shaking the pan until lightly browned all over. Leave to cool then very roughly chop.

Using an electric mixer, whisk the eggs, sugar and vanilla essence together until they are very thick and a trail is left when the whisk is lifted out of the mixture. Gradually fold in the melted butter and chocolate. Sift the flour and baking powder over the top then gently fold in until just mixed. Fold in half the nuts.

Pour the mixture into the lined tin, tilt to ease the mixture into the corners then sprinkle with the remaining nuts. Bake for about 25 minutes, checking after 20 minutes, until the top is crusty and cracked and the centre is still soft and squidgy. If unsure, insert a small, fine-bladed knife into the centre – it should come out slightly smeared with chocolate. Too long in the oven and the brownies will be dry and very set. Leave to cool and harden slightly in the tin.

Lift the paper out of the tin, spoon the melted chocolate over the top of the brownies in random zigzag lines, leave to set for 15 minutes or so and then cut into 24 squares.

Tip If you are not a fan of nuts, add 100 g (3½ oz) diced white or milk chocolate or a sprinkling of ready chopped stoned dates instead.

Chocolate macaroons

These dainty, Parisian-style macaroons are crisp on the outside with a soft, slightly chewy centre.

Makes 20
Preparation time:
  30 minutes + 1 hour
  chilling + cooling
Cooking time:
  15–18 minutes

25 g (1 oz) cocoa powder
150 g (5½ oz) icing sugar
100 g (3½ oz) ground almonds
3 egg whites
a pinch of salt
75 g (2¾ oz) caster sugar
icing sugar, sifted, to decorate

Chocolate ganache filling
100 ml (3½ fl oz) double cream
100 g (3½ oz) dark chocolate
  (70% cocoa), broken into pieces

Preheat the oven to 160°C/325°F/Gas Mark 3. Line two baking sheets with non-stick baking paper and draw 2.5 cm (1 inch) circles on the underside of the paper using a tiny biscuit cutter or base of a glass as a guide.

Blend the cocoa powder, icing sugar and ground almonds together in a food processor or liquidiser then sift into a bowl.

Whisk the egg whites and salt with an electric mixer until they form stiff, moist-looking peaks then gradually whisk in the caster sugar a teaspoonful at a time until the meringue is stiff and glossy.

Gently fold in the cocoa mixture with a large serving spoon until evenly mixed then spoon into a large nylon piping bag fitted with a 1 cm (½ inch) plain piping nozzle. Pipe circles on the paper-lined baking sheets then leave at room temperature for 10 minutes.

Transfer the baking sheets to the oven and bake for 15–18 minutes until the macaroons are firm on the outside and may be easily peeled off the paper. Leave to cool on the paper.

To make the filling, bring the cream just to the boil in a small saucepan. Take off the heat, add the chocolate pieces and leave until melted. Stir until smooth then cover with cling film and chill for 1 hour or until stiff. Stir once more and use to sandwich the macaroons in pairs. Arrange on a plate and decorate with sifted icing sugar to serve.

Tips The macaroon shells can be made the day before they are needed, or even 2 days before, and kept in a biscuit tin lined with non-stick baking paper. Fill with chocolate ganache no more than 2 hours before serving or they will go very soft.

Instead of chocolate ganache, you could cheat with a little chocolate and hazelnut spread or some whipped cream flavoured with a little orange zest or peppermint essence. They also look very pretty if, once filled, they are rolled in very finely chopped pistachio nuts so that the nuts coat the filling, or if a tiny sugared viola or pansy flower is pressed on to the cream.

No-bake chocolate cake

Perhaps not a cake in the truest sense, these seriously chocolatey squares are made by melting the ingredients together rather than baking.

Cuts into 25 squares
Preparation time:
 15 minutes +
 10 minutes cooling +
 2–3 hours chilling

100 g (3½ oz) butter
100 g (3½ oz) dark chocolate
 (70% cocoa), broken into pieces
100 g (3½ oz) milk chocolate
 (32% cocoa), broken into pieces
3 tablespoons golden syrup
150 g (5½ oz) malted milk biscuits
50 g (1¾ oz) pistachios, halved
 (optional)
135 g (4¾ oz) Maltesers
100 g (3½ oz) mini pink and white
 marshmallows

Put the butter, dark and milk chocolate and golden syrup in a large mixing bowl and set it over a saucepan of gently simmering water. Leave until melted, stirring only occasionally.

Meanwhile, cut a square of non-stick baking paper a little larger than a shallow 20 cm (8 inch) cake tin, snip into the corners diagonally then press the paper into the tin so that the base and sides are lined.

Break the biscuits into rough pieces with your fingertips and stir into the chocolate mixture with the pistachios, if using. Take the bowl off the heat and allow to cool for 10 minutes or so.

Stir the Maltesers and marshmallows into the chocolate mixture then spoon into the lined tin and press into an even layer. Chill in the fridge for 2–3 hours until firm, then lift the paper from the tin, cut the cake into small squares and lift off the paper to serve.

Tip Don't be tempted to stir the Maltesers and marshmallows into the hot chocolate mix along with the biscuits or the chocolate will fall off the sweets and the marshmallows will melt and lose their shape.

Millionaire shortbread

A crumbly, butter shortbread topped with a toffee layer then a rich dark chocolate frosting. A timeless favourite that is loved by all ages.

Cuts into 12 bars
Preparation time:
   25 minutes + cooling +
   chilling
Cooking time:
   20–25 minutes

Shortbread base
225 g (8 oz) plain flour
25 g (1 oz) cornflour
75 g (2¾ oz) caster sugar
175 g (6 oz) butter, diced

Toffee layer
50 g (1¾ oz) butter
75 g (2¾ oz) dark muscovado
   sugar
400 ml (14 fl oz) can full fat
   condensed milk

Chocolate frosting
25 g (1 oz) butter
100 g (3½ oz) dark chocolate
   (70% cocoa), broken into pieces
25 g (1 oz) icing sugar, sifted
2–3 teaspoons milk

Preheat the oven to 180°C/350°F/Gas Mark 4. Line a shallow 20 cm (8 inch) square cake tin with a large piece of non-stick baking paper, snip into the corners diagonally then press the paper into the tin so that the base and sides are lined.

For the base, put the flour, cornflour and sugar into a bowl, add the butter and rub in with your fingertips or an electric mixer until the mixture looks like fine crumbs. Squeeze the crumbs together with your hands until a ball is formed.

Press the dough into the base of the lined tin, prick with a fork then bake for 20–25 minutes until pale golden around the edges. Take out of the oven and leave to cool for a while.

To make the toffee layer, heat the butter and sugar in a medium saucepan until the butter has melted and the sugar has dissolved. Add the condensed milk and cook over a low heat, stirring constantly for 3 minutes until the mixture begins to smell of toffee and thicken slightly. Pour over the shortbread and ease into an even layer. Leave to cool and harden.

To make the frosting, put the butter and chocolate into a bowl set over a saucepan of gently simmering water and leave to melt. Sift the sugar over and stir until melted. Mix in enough milk to make a smooth spreadable icing.

Spoon the frosting over the toffee and shortbread in the tin, ease into a smooth layer with the back of the spoon then swirl with a knife to make a decorative pattern. Leave to cool then chill until the chocolate layer is firm. Lift the shortbread out of the tin using the paper, peel the paper away and cut the shortbread into 12 bars.

Tips For an extra chocolatey taste, substitute 25 g (1 oz) of the plain flour for cocoa powder.

These will keep in a biscuit tin for 3–4 days.

Choc chip and banana loaf

This is a great way to use up those bananas languishing in the fruit bowl. It stores well, so just cut off a slice when you need it and add it to a lunchbox.

Cuts into 10 slices
Preparation time:
  25 minutes + cooling
Cooking time: 1–1¼ hours

100 g (3½ oz) butter, at room temperature, plus extra for greasing
3 small ripe bananas (400 g/14 oz with skins)
1 tablespoon lemon juice
150 g (5½ oz) caster sugar
2 eggs
250 g (9 oz) self-raising flour
1 teaspoon baking powder
2 tablespoons milk
150 g (5½ oz) Swiss milk chocolate, diced

Preheat the oven to 160°C/325°F/Gas Mark 3. Grease a 900 g (2 lb) loaf tin and line the two long sides and base with a piece of greaseproof or non-stick baking paper.

Peel the bananas and mash with the lemon juice.

Cream the butter and sugar together in a bowl. Add the eggs, bananas, flour and baking powder and mix until smooth then stir in the milk to make a soft dropping consistency.

Spoon one-third of the mixture into the tin and sprinkle with one-third of the chocolate. Repeat the layers then finish with the remaining banana mixture. Smooth the top level. Reserve the last third of chocolate for later.

Bake for 1–1¼ hours or until well risen, the top is golden and cracked and a skewer comes out clean when inserted into the centre of the loaf. Leave to cool in the tin for 20 minutes then loosen the edges and turn out on to a wire rack. Sprinkle with the remaining chocolate and leave to cool. Peel off the lining paper and cut into thick slices to serve.

Whoopies

These little cakes, sometimes known as 'pies', are the latest American craze and might even become more popular than the much loved muffin.

Makes 20
Preparation time:
  45 minutes
Cooking time:
  10–12 minutes

40 g (1½ oz) cocoa powder
4 tablespoons boiling water
250 g (9 oz) plain flour
1 teaspoon baking powder
2 teaspoons bicarbonate of soda
175 g (6 oz) light muscovado
  sugar
75 g (2¾ oz) butter, melted
150 g (5½ oz) natural yogurt
1 egg

Peanut and cream cheese
  filling

75 g (2¾ oz) salted peanuts
200 g (7 oz) cream cheese
200 g (7 oz) icing sugar, sifted

Chocolate frosting

100 g (3½ oz) dark chocolate
  (70% cocoa), broken into pieces
2–4 tablespoons milk
50 g (1¾ oz) icing sugar, sifted

Preheat the oven to 200°C/400°F/Gas Mark 6. Line three baking sheets with non-stick baking paper.

Mix the cocoa powder and boiling water together until you get a smooth paste.

Put the flour, baking powder, bicarbonate of soda and sugar into a mixing bowl and stir together. Add the cocoa paste, butter, yogurt and egg and beat together until smooth.

Pipe or spoon the mixture into fourty 5 cm (2 inch) rounds on the baking sheets, leaving space between for them to rise during baking. Leave to stand for 5 minutes.

Bake for 10–12 minutes until risen, the tops are cracked, the outside is crusty, the centre still slightly soft and the cakes can be lifted easily off the paper. Leave to cool on the paper then transfer half the cakes to a wire rack and set this over a tray.

Meanwhile, make the filling by whizzing the peanuts in a liquidiser or food processor until they are finely chopped. Beat the cream cheese and icing sugar together until just smooth then stir in the peanuts, reserving a small amount for decoration. Chill until needed.

To make the frosting, melt the chocolate with 2 tablespoons of milk in a bowl set over a saucepan of gently simmering water. Take off the heat then add the icing sugar and stir until smooth, mixing in a little extra milk if needed to make a coating consistency. Spoon the frosting over the biscuits on the wire rack then sprinkle with the reserved peanuts. Leave to set.

To finish, pipe or spoon the cream cheese filling on to the underside of the plain cakes then top with the iced cakes. Transfer to a serving plate.

Tips In true American style, these have been filled with a peanut and cream cheese filling but, for something a little more conservative, you may want to try flavouring them with a little grated orange zest and juice, some vanilla or ground cinnamon.

You could finish these dainty cakes with a homemade piped chocolate shape (see page 9), piped zig zag lines of melted white or milk chocolate or bought sugar flowers.

Chilled desserts

Spiced chocolate pavlovas

Everyone thinks of summer berry pavlovas, but these blackberry-topped, chocolate-swirled pavlovas make a great autumn alternative.

Serves 6
Preparation time:
  35 minutes
Cooking time: 1–1¼ hours

100 g (3½ oz) dark chocolate
  (70% cocoa), broken into pieces
3 egg whites
175 g (6 oz) golden (or white)
  caster sugar
1 teaspoon cornflour
1 teaspoon white wine vinegar
¼ teaspoon ground cinnamon

To decorate
225 g (8 oz) frozen blackberries
  (or pick your own if in season)
50 g (1¾ oz) golden (or white)
  caster sugar
4 tablespoons water
250 ml (9 fl oz) double cream

Preheat the oven to 110°C/225°F/Gas Mark ¼.

Melt the chocolate in a bowl set over a saucepan of gently simmering water.

Whisk the egg whites in a large bowl until they form stiff, moist peaks then gradually whisk in the sugar a teaspoonful at a time. Continue whisking for a minute or two more until the meringue is thick and glossy.

Mix the cornflour with the vinegar then fold into the meringue with the cinnamon. Add the chocolate and swirl together until partially mixed for a marbled effect.

Spoon six rough-shaped mounds on to a large baking sheet lined with non-stick baking paper. Spread each to about 10 cm (4 inches) in diameter and make a slight dip in the centre of each.

Bake for 1–1¼ hours or until the meringues can be easily peeled off the paper. Take out of the oven and leave to cool on the paper.

Put the blackberries, sugar and water in a small saucepan and heat gently for 5 minutes until softened. Leave to cool. Whip the cream until it forms soft peaks then spoon on to the pavlovas and transfer to individual serving plates. Spoon the blackberries over the top and serve immediately.

Tips If you have a bottle of crème de cassis in the cupboard, use a little of this in place of the water in the blackberry compote.

The pavlovas may be made up to 2 days in advance and stored layered between non-stick baking paper in a large biscuit tin. Once topped with cream, serve within 1 hour, adding the blackberries at the very last minute.

Blueberry crème brûlées

We often order crème brûlée when out in a restaurant, but how many of us actually make them at home? Don't be put off – it's surprisingly easy.

Serves 4
Preparation time:
  25 minutes + 3–4 hours chilling + cooling
Cooking time:
  20–25 minutes

300 ml (10 fl oz) **double cream**
100 g (3½ oz) **white chocolate,** broken into pieces
4 **egg yolks**
25 g (1 oz) **caster sugar,** plus 2 tablespoons for sprinkling
100 g (3½ oz) **fresh blueberries**

Preheat the oven to 180°C/350°F/Gas Mark 4.

Pour the cream into a saucepan and bring just to the boil. Take it off the heat, add the chocolate and leave for 5 minutes, stirring very occasionally until melted.

Whisk the egg yolks and sugar together until just mixed then gradually whisk in the warm cream mixture. Pour through a sieve back into the saucepan.

Divide the blueberries between four 150 ml (5 fl oz) ovenproof ramekin dishes and stand the dishes in a small roasting tin. Pour the custard into the dishes (the blueberries will float) then pour hot water from the tap into the roasting tin to come halfway up the sides of the dishes. Cook, uncovered, in the oven for 20–25 minutes until the desserts are just set with a slight softness to the centre.

Lift the dishes out of the tin with a cloth, leave to cool then chill in the fridge for 3–4 hours or until ready to serve.

Sprinkle the tops liberally with the remaining sugar then light a cook's torch and, holding it about 7.5 cm (3 inches) away from the sugar, gently move the torch over the top of one of the desserts until the sugar has dissolved. Continue heating until the top is golden brown then repeat with the other desserts. Leave for 5 minutes for the sugar to harden then serve within 30–40 minutes.

Tip If you don't have a cook's torch, stand the dishes in a small shallow cake tin, pack ice cubes around the dishes so that the custard stays cool, sprinkle the sugar over the top and cook under a hot grill until the sugar has dissolved and caramelised. Leave for a few minutes to harden then take the dishes out of the ice and serve.

Chocolate crème caramels

Richer and more luxurious than its plain vanilla cousin, this dark chocolate custard may be preferred by those who find dark chocolate mousse a little rich.

Serves 6
Preparation time:
  20 minutes + 3–4 hours chilling + cooling
Cooking time:
  30–35 minutes

150 g (5½ oz) granulated sugar
4 tablespoons boiling water
450 ml (16 fl oz) full fat or
  semi-skimmed milk
150 ml (5 fl oz) double cream
150 g (5½ oz) dark chocolate
  (70% cocoa), broken into pieces
1 teaspoon instant coffee
  granules or powder
2 eggs
2 egg yolks
50 g (1¾ oz) caster sugar
chocolate shavings, to decorate

Preheat the oven to 160°C/325°F/Gas Mark 3.

Put the granulated sugar in a saucepan with 125 ml (4½ fl oz) of water and heat very gently, without stirring, until the sugar has dissolved. Raise the heat and boil the syrup until it has turned golden brown. This will take about 5 minutes and the syrup will begin to slowly colour around the edges. Once this happens keep a very close eye on the pan as the colour will quickly move to the centre of the pan and, if left, change to a very dark brown.

Take the pan off the heat and immediately add the boiling water, a tablespoon at a time. Stand well back between each addition as the syrup will spit. Tilt the pan to mix the syrup then pour immediately into six 200 ml (7 fl oz) metal pudding moulds. Tilt the moulds so that the syrup coats the sides and bases evenly then stand the moulds in a roasting tin.

Pour the milk and cream into a saucepan then bring just to the boil. Turn off the heat and add the chocolate and instant coffee. Leave to stand for about 10 minutes, stirring occasionally until the chocolate has melted.

Whisk the eggs, egg yolks and caster sugar together until just mixed. Gradually whisk in the warm chocolate milk until smooth then pour the mixture through a sieve back into the pan. Divide the custard between the caramel-lined moulds then pour hot water from the tap into the roasting tin to come halfway up the sides of the pudding moulds.

Transfer to the oven and cook uncovered for 30–35 minutes or until the puddings are set when lightly pressed in the centre with a fingertip. Lift the moulds out of the roasting tin with a cloth, leave to cool then chill in the fridge for 3–4 hours.

To serve, dip the moulds into a bowl of just boiled water, count to 10, then lift all the moulds out of the water. Loosen the top edge of the custard with a wetted fingertip then invert one mould at a time on to a small plate. Holding the mould and plate, jerk to release the pudding then remove the mould. Decorate with chocolate shavings and serve immediately.

Double chocolate tart

Don't skimp on quality – this is only as good as the chocolate used. Serve at room temperature with vanilla ice cream and a dusting of cocoa powder.

Serves 8
Preparation time:
  30 minutes + 15 minutes
  chilling + 2 hours cooling
  + 15 minutes setting
Cooking time: 35 minutes

75 g (2¾ oz) white chocolate, melted, to decorate

Pastry case
165 g (5¾ oz) plain flour, plus extra for dusting
15 g (½ oz) cocoa powder
50 g (1¾ oz) caster sugar
75 g (2¾ oz) butter, diced, plus extra for greasing
2 egg yolks

Chocolate filling
2 eggs, beaten
300 ml (10 fl oz) double cream
200 ml (7 fl oz) milk
200 g (7 oz) dark chocolate (70% cocoa), broken into pieces
75 g (2¾ oz) caster sugar

Preheat the oven to 190°C/375°F/Gas Mark 5.

To make the pastry, put the flour, cocoa powder and sugar in a bowl, add the butter and rub in with your fingertips or an electric mixer until the mixture looks like fine crumbs. Add the egg yolks and a little cold water to mix to a smooth dough.

Grease a 25 cm (10 inch) wide, 2.5 cm (1 inch) deep, loose-bottomed fluted flan tin. Knead the pastry lightly on a lightly floured surface then roll out until large enough to line the tin. Trim the top of the pastry so that it is 5 mm (¼ inch) above the top of the tin. Prick the base, put on a baking sheet then chill for 15 minutes.

Line the pastry case with a piece of greaseproof or non-stick baking paper and fill with baking beans. Bake for 10 minutes. Remove the paper and beans and cook for 5 minutes more then brush the inside of the case with a little of the beaten eggs for the filling and cook for another 5 minutes.

Meanwhile, bring the cream and milk just to the boil in a saucepan. Take off the heat, add the chocolate and leave until melted. Stir until smooth, warming the milk if needed.

Lightly whisk the rest of the eggs and the sugar together. Gradually whisk in the chocolate mix.

Reduce the oven temperature to 160°C/325°F/Gas Mark 3. Pull the oven shelf holding the pastry case out slightly, pour the chocolate mix into the case then gently slide the oven shelf back in. Cook for about 15 minutes until the edges of the filling are set and beginning to crack and the centre has a soft wobble (it will firm up as it cools). Leave to cool at room temperature for at least 2 hours.

Take the tart out of the tin, put on a serving plate and decorate with piped lines of melted white chocolate. Leave to harden for 15 minutes then cut into wedges.

Tip Brushing inside the just-cooked pastry case with beaten egg helps to seal any cracks in the pastry so that the filling does not run out during baking.

Chilli cardamom sorbet

It can be tricky to know what to serve after spicy food. This refreshing, Aztec-inspired sorbet will cool things down and makes a great standby.

Serves 6
Preparation time:
  25 minutes + 30 minutes
  in an ice cream machine
  or 4–6 hours freezing
Cooking time:
  15 minutes

250 g (9 oz) caster sugar
100 g (3½ oz) cocoa powder
4–6 cardamom pods, depending
  on size, crushed
½–1 red bird's eye chilli,
  deseeded but not chopped,
  to taste

Tuile biscuits
1 egg white
50 g (1¾ oz) caster sugar
25 g (1 oz) butter, melted
25 g (1 oz) plain flour, sifted
2 drops vanilla essence
1 teaspoon cocoa powder, sifted

Put 600 ml (20 fl oz) of water and the sugar in a saucepan and bring slowly to the boil. Add the cocoa powder, crushed cardamom pods and their seeds and the chilli and stir until the cocoa has dissolved. Simmer gently for 10 minutes, stirring occasionally until the mixture is syrupy. Leave to cool then strain.

Pour the mixture into an ice cream machine and churn for 30 minutes or until thick and firm enough to scoop. Transfer to the freezer until ready to serve. Alternatively, pour the syrup into a small non-stick cake tin or roasting tin and freeze for 4–6 hours, beating two or three times when semi frozen to break up the ice crystals. Return to the freezer for several hours or overnight until firm.

Meanwhile, make the biscuits. Heat the oven to 200°C/400°F/Gas Mark 6 and line two baking sheets with non-stick baking paper. Fork the egg white and sugar together in a bowl until just mixed. Add the melted butter, flour and vanilla essence and fork together until smooth.

Transfer 1 tablespoon of the mixture to a cup and mix in the sifted cocoa powder until smooth. Spoon into a greaseproof paper piping bag and fold the top down to enclose.

Drop teaspoons of the plain biscuit mixture on to the paper-lined baking sheets to make 12 biscuits then spread very thinly so each is about 7.5 cm (3 inches) in diameter. Snip the tip off the end of the piping bag then pipe hearts, names, initials or a pattern on to each biscuit. Bake for 4–6 minutes until pale golden around the edges then leave to cool on the paper.

When ready to serve, take the sorbet out of the freezer and leave to soften at room temperature for 10 minutes or until soft enough to scoop. Spoon into small glasses and serve with the biscuits.

Tip The chocolate mixture can be piped over the biscuits in zigzag lines and the biscuits cooked, just three or four at a time, on a tray lined with non-stick baking paper. When baked, leave for a few seconds then lift off the paper and wrap around the handle of a wooden spoon. When cool slide off the spoon for a biscuit known as a cigarette russe. Try shaping larger biscuits over an orange. When cool, spoon the sorbet into the biscuit cups. Don't try to cook and shape too many at a time or they will have set before you can shape them. They can also be made without the cocoa and half dipped into melted chocolate after baking.

Two-tone cheesecake

A rich, American-style, baked vanilla cheesecake marbled with a dark chocolate layer and encased in a milk chocolate biscuit case.

Serves 8–10
Preparation time:
  40 minutes + cooling +
  overnight chilling
Cooking time:
  35–40 minutes

Biscuit base
75 g (2¾ oz) **butter**, plus extra for greasing
250 g (9 oz) **milk chocolate digestive biscuits**

Chocolate cheesecake
200 g (7 oz) **dark chocolate (70% cocoa)**, broken into pieces
600 g (1 lb 5 oz) **medium-fat soft cheese**
100 g (3½ oz) **caster sugar**
1 teaspoon **vanilla essence**
4 **eggs**
200 ml (7 fl oz) **double cream**

Preheat the oven to 180°C/350°F/Gas Mark 4.

Melt the butter in a medium saucepan. Crush the biscuits in a plastic bag using a rolling pin or blitz in a food processor. Stir into the melted butter then tip into a buttered 23 cm (9 inch) springform tin. Press the crumbs into the base of the tin with the end of a rolling pin.

Bake for 5 minutes to set the crust then take out of the oven and reduce the temperature to 150°C/300°F/Gas Mark 2.

Meanwhile, melt the chocolate in a bowl set over a saucepan of gently simmering water. Put the cream cheese into a bowl, add the sugar and vanilla essence and mix briefly until smooth. Gradually mix in the eggs, one at a time, until smooth, then stir in the double cream and whisk for a minute or two until thick.

Ladle 300 ml (10 fl oz) of the mixture into a measuring jug. Gradually stir into the melted chocolate until smooth. Spoon half the remaining cheesecake mixture on to the biscuit case then spoon over half the chocolate mixture, filling any gaps.

Continue adding alternate teaspoonfuls of the vanilla and chocolate mixtures then, using the handle of a teaspoon, swirl the two mixtures together to give a marbled effect. Don't worry too much if the top is uneven.

Bake for 35–40 minutes or until the cheesecake is set around the edges, lightly cracked and still slightly soft in the centre. Turn the oven off, open the door and leave ajar for 1 hour. Take the cheesecake out, cool completely then transfer to the fridge overnight.

Loosen the edge of the cheesecake with a knife, remove the tin, transfer to a serving plate and cut into wedges to serve.

Tip This cheesecake can be frozen successfully as soon as it is cool. Open freeze out of the tin until firm then wrap in cling film and protect in a plastic box. Seal, label and freeze up to 6 weeks. Unwrap and defrost overnight in the fridge.

Chocolate love hearts

A twist on chocolate éclairs, the chocolate pastry is piped into heart shapes and filled with softly whipped cream flavoured with raspberries and mint.

Makes 8
Preparation time:
40 minutes + 15 minutes setting
Cooking time:
13–15 minutes

50 g (1¾ oz) butter, plus extra for greasing
50 g (1¾ oz) plain flour
15 g (½ oz) cocoa powder
a pinch of salt
25 g (1 oz) caster sugar
2 eggs, beaten
½ teaspoon vanilla essence

To finish
250 ml (8 fl oz) double cream
100 g (3½ oz) frozen raspberries, defrosted
2 tablespoons icing sugar
1 tablespoon chopped fresh mint
75 g (2¾ oz) dark chocolate (70% cocoa)
15 g (½ oz) butter
white chocolate shavings (optional)

Put the butter and 150 ml (5 fl oz) of water in a small saucepan and bring slowly to the boil so that the butter melts. Take the pan off the heat and sift in the flour, cocoa powder and salt. Add the sugar and return the pan to the heat. Stir constantly with a wooden spoon until the mixture makes a smooth ball. Leave to cool.

Preheat the oven to 210°C/425°F/Gas Mark 7. Gradually beat the eggs and vanilla essence into the choux pastry and continue to beat until smooth.

Spoon the mixture into a nylon piping bag fitted with a 1 cm (½ inch) plain piping nozzle and pipe eight 7.5 cm (3 inch) long heart shapes on to two greased baking sheets.

Place in the oven, reduce the heat to 200°C/400°F/ Gas Mark 6 and cook for 13–15 minutes until well risen and crisp.

Using a serrated knife, cut each heart in half and arrange cut sides uppermost on the baking sheets to cool.

Whip the cream until it forms soft peaks then fold in the raspberries and any juices, half the sugar and the mint and mix briefly so that the raspberries marble the cream. Spoon over the lower heart shapes then cover with the tops.

Melt the chocolate, butter and remaining icing sugar in a bowl set over a saucepan of gently simmering water, stirring occasionally until smooth. Spoon over the heart shapes and sprinkle with the white chocolate shavings, if using. Leave for 15 minutes for the frosting to harden then serve.

Tip It is always important to measure ingredients accurately, but choux pastry is one of those recipes where measurements are crucial. Not enough flour and the mixture will be too soft to pipe, too much and it will be firm and hard when cooked.

Chocolate banoffee pie

With some melted chocolate in the filling and milk chocolate digestives for the base, this favourite pudding is lifted up to a new level.

Serves 8
Preparation time:
  40 minutes + 15 minutes chilling + 1 hour setting

Biscuit base
75 g (2¾ oz) butter
250 g (9 oz) milk chocolate
   digestive biscuits

Banoffee topping
75 g (2¾ oz) butter
75 g (2¾ oz) dark muscovado
   sugar
400 g (14 oz) can full fat
   condensed milk
75 g (2¾ oz) dark chocolate
   (70% cocoa), broken into pieces
300 ml (10 fl oz) double cream
3 small bananas
juice of 1 lemon

To decorate
50 g (1¾ oz) dark chocolate
   (70% cocoa), melted
white chocolate curls

For the base, melt the butter in a medium saucepan. Crush the biscuits in a plastic bag using a rolling pin or in a food processor then stir into the butter until well coated. Tip into a 24 cm (9½ inch) loose-bottomed, fluted flan tin and press firmly into the base and up the sides. Chill for 15 minutes.

Wash and dry the pan then heat the butter and sugar for the topping until both have melted. Add the condensed milk and cook over a medium heat for 2–3 minutes, stirring constantly, until the mixture is just beginning to thicken and smell of toffee.

Take the pan off the heat and add the dark chocolate. Stir until melted then pour into the biscuit case. Leave to cool and set at room temperature for 1 hour.

Lift the biscuit case out of the tin and transfer to a serving plate. Whip the cream until it forms soft swirls. Slice the bananas and toss in the lemon juice. Fold two-thirds of the bananas into the cream and spoon over the toffee layer. Arrange the remaining bananas on top then drizzle with the melted dark chocolate and sprinkle with the chocolate curls. This is best served up to 3 hours after decorating.

Tip Don't want to make chocolate curls? Sprinkle with a little grated dark chocolate or a light dusting of sifted cocoa powder.

Dark chocolate mousse

Chocolate mousse is one of those wonderfully quick desserts. This one is made special by the addition of a light tangy syllabub cream.

Serves 6
Preparation time:
  25 minutes + 3–4 hours
  chilling + cooling
Cooking time: 10 minutes

200 g (7 oz) dark chocolate (70% cocoa), broken into pieces
15 g (½ oz) butter
4 tablespoons icing sugar
3 eggs, separated
finely grated zest and juice of 1 large orange
150 ml (5 fl oz) double cream
1 tablespoon brandy or orange-flavoured liqueur
sifted cocoa powder, to decorate
tuile biscuits (see page 38) or tiny shop bought biscuits, to serve

Put the chocolate and butter in a large bowl and set over a saucepan of gently simmering water. Leave for 10 minutes, stirring occasionally, until the chocolate has melted.

Add 2 tablespoons of icing sugar to the chocolate then gradually beat in the egg yolks, one at a time until smooth. Mix in half the orange zest and 3 tablespoons of the orange juice then take the bowl off the heat. Wrap the remaining orange zest in foil for later.

Whisk the egg whites until they form moist peaks then fold a spoonful into the chocolate mixture to loosen it slightly. Add the remaining egg whites and fold in gently until just mixed. Spoon into six small glasses or coffee cups, leave to cool then transfer to the fridge for 3–4 hours until set.

When almost ready to serve, pour the cream into a bowl, add the remaining orange zest and icing sugar and whisk until the cream softly holds its shape. Gradually whisk in 3 tablespoons of orange juice and then the brandy or liqueur. Whisk for a minute or two more until softly spoonable. Spoon on to the tops of the mousses, dust lightly with cocoa powder and serve with biscuits.

Tip When melting chocolate, check that the bottom of the bowl does not come into contact with the water and keep the heat as low as possible so that the water gently simmers and the chocolate does not overheat. If it does, you may find that the chocolate 'seizes' or sets firm the minute that the egg yolks are added, which can spoil the texture of the finished mousse.

Triple chocolate parfait

This French-style ice cream is made with a boiled sugar syrup. Serve as it is or with a little warm Maple and chocolate sauce (see page 14).

Serves 6–8
Preparation time:
  40 minutes + overnight freezing

100 g (3½ oz) dark chocolate
  (70% cocoa), broken into pieces
100 g (3½ oz) milk chocolate
  (32% cocoa), broken into pieces
100 g (3½ oz) white chocolate,
  broken into pieces
200 g (7 oz) caster sugar
6 egg yolks
450 ml (16 fl oz) double cream
dark and white chocolate curls,
  to decorate

Melt the chocolates in three separate bowls (see Tip).

Put the sugar and 200 ml (7 fl oz) of water in a saucepan and heat gently, without stirring, until the sugar has dissolved.

Meanwhile, put the egg yolks in a large bowl. One-third fill a large saucepan with water and bring to a gentle simmer, but do not put the bowl on the pan just yet.

Increase the heat and boil the sugar syrup until it reaches 115°C (239°F) on a sugar thermometer or until a little of the syrup will make a soft ball when dropped into a glass of cold water. If the syrup forms brittle strands that snap when lifted out of the water, the syrup is too hot and it will need to be remade; if it is too soft to make a ball then it is not quite hot enough. If testing in cold water, take the pan off the heat while waiting for the syrup to cool in the water, but as a rough guide the syrup will begin to fall slowly off a spoon when it is almost ready.

As soon as the soft ball stage is reached, quickly take the pan off the heat, remove the thermometer, place the egg yolks over the simmering water then gradually whisk the hot sugar syrup into the yolks in a thin steady stream. Continue to whisk until the yolks are very thick and the mixture leaves a trail when the whisk is lifted above it.

Take the bowl off the heat and whisk for a few more minutes until the mixture is beginning to cool. Whisk the cream until it forms soft swirls then fold into the egg mixture. Divide the mixture into three equal-sized amounts then fold each into a different bowl of chocolate.

Line a 900 g (2 lb) loaf tin with a large piece of cling film then pour in the white chocolate mixture. Freeze for 15 minutes until partially set, leaving the other mixtures at room temperature.

Spoon the milk chocolate mixture over the white and spread gently into an even layer. Freeze for 15 minutes, leaving the dark chocolate mixture still at room temperature. Spoon over the final layer then freeze the parfait overnight until firm.

About 10 minutes before serving, loosen the parfait by lifting the cling film a little then cover the tin with a plate, turn the plate and tin over, lift off the tin and peel away the cling film. Decorate the top with dark and white chocolate curls and cut into thick slices with a hot knife.

Tip Rather than melting the chocolates above a saucepan of gently simmering water, you may prefer to melt them in the microwave. Use small microwaveproof bowls and set the microwave to full power. Melt the dark chocolate for 1 minute then leave to stand, then the milk chocolate for 1 minute and leave to stand. White chocolate has a tendency to burn in the microwave, so heat for 30 seconds first on medium power, check then continue in 10 second bursts until it is softened then stir. Melt the dark and milk chocolate for an extra 10 seconds each if needed, then stir.

Hot puddings

Bread and butter pudding

Made with chocolate, pecan nuts and a vanilla and cinnamon spiced custard. Serve with maple syrup and cream to banish the winter blues.

Serves 4
Preparation time:
 15 minutes + 1 hour soaking
Cooking time:
 30–35 minutes

40 g (1½ oz) **butter**, plus extra for greasing
400 g (14 oz) **day-old white bread**, cut into 2.5 cm (1 inch) cubes, crusts left on
100 g (3½ oz) **milk chocolate (39% cocoa)**, diced
50 g (1¾ oz) **pecan nuts**, roughly broken
3 **eggs**
75 g (2¾ oz) **caster sugar**
1 teaspoon **vanilla essence**
1 teaspoon **ground cinnamon**
450 ml (16 fl oz) **milk**

To serve
icing sugar, sifted
maple syrup
double cream

Butter a 1.5 litre (2¾ pint) shallow, ovenproof dish. Scatter over the bread, chocolate and nuts.

Whisk the eggs, sugar, vanilla essence, cinnamon and milk together in a jug then strain over the bread, pressing the mixture through the sieve with a spoon so that all the bread is coated with the milk. Cover loosely with foil and leave to stand for at least 1 hour.

Preheat the oven to 180°C/350°F/Gas Mark 4.

Remove the foil and dot the top of the bread with the butter. Bake for 30–35 minutes until the pudding is golden and the custard just set. (Check after 20–25 minutes and cover loosely with foil for the remaining cooking time if it looks like the pudding is browning too quickly.)

Dust the top lightly with sifted icing sugar then spoon into bowls and serve warm drizzled with maple syrup and a little cream.

White choc orange soufflés

Partly make this in advance so that you only need to whisk and fold in the egg whites and white chocolate at the very last minute.

Serves 4
Preparation time:
  30 minutes
Cooking time:
  10–12 minutes

butter, for greasing
75 g (2¾ oz) caster sugar, plus
  4 teaspoons for soufflé dishes
3 egg yolks
40 g (1½ oz) plain flour
250 ml (9 fl oz) milk
grated zest of ½ a small orange
5 egg whites
150 g (5½ oz) white chocolate,
  finely diced
icing sugar, sifted, to decorate

Brandied chocolate sauce
100 g (3½ oz) dark chocolate
  (70% cocoa), broken into pieces
4 tablespoons milk
2 tablespoons brandy or Grand
  Marnier
caster sugar, for sprinkling

Butter the inside of four 10 cm (4 inch) diameter and 6 cm (2½ inch) deep soufflé dishes. Sprinkle each with a teaspoon of sugar and tilt the dishes to coat the insides.

Whisk the egg yolks and caster sugar together in a bowl for a few minutes until thick and pale. Sift the flour over the top and fold in.

Pour the milk into a saucepan, bring just to the boil then gradually whisk into the egg yolk mixture until smooth. Pour back into the saucepan and cook over a medium heat, stirring constantly until very thick and smooth. Stir in the orange zest then cover with a piece of wetted greaseproof paper and leave to cool.

To make the sauce, put the chocolate and milk into a small saucepan and cook over a low heat, stirring occasionally until the chocolate has melted. Stir in the brandy or Grand Marnier. Sprinkle the surface with a little extra sugar so that a skin doesn't form and set aside until needed.

When almost ready to serve, preheat the oven to 210°C/425°F/Gas Mark 7.

Whisk the egg whites until they form stiff, moist-looking peaks. Beat the orange mixture once to soften then stir in the white chocolate. Fold in a spoonful of the egg white to loosen the mixture then gently fold in the remainder.

Divide the soufflé mixture gently between the dishes, stand them on a baking sheet and cook for 10–12 minutes until well risen and golden. While they cook, warm the chocolate sauce, pour into four small dishes or egg cups and set these on four large plates. As soon as the soufflés are ready, transfer the dishes to the serving plates, dust the tops with a little sifted icing sugar and serve immediately.

Tip As soon as you take the soufflés out of the oven they will begin losing volume, so make sure that your guests are ready and waiting.

White chocolate risotto

Luxuriously smooth, risotto rice has a uniquely creamy taste. Buy the best white chocolate you can and use a whole vanilla pod for a superior flavour.

Serves 4
Preparation time:
10 minutes
Cooking time: 30 minutes

1 litre (1¾ pints) semi-skimmed
   milk
40 g (1½ oz) butter
200 g (7 oz) risotto rice
1 vanilla pod, split lengthways
6 tablespoons Pineau des
   Charentes or white dessert
   wine
50 g (1¾ oz) caster sugar
100 g (3½ oz) white chocolate,
   broken into pieces
150 ml (5 fl oz) boiling water

To serve
225 g (8 oz) small strawberries,
   halved
dark chocolate, grated
clotted cream or crème fraîche

Pour the milk into a saucepan and bring just to the boil.

Melt the butter in a frying pan then add the rice and stir until coated in the butter.

Scrape the seeds from the vanilla pod then add the seeds and pod to the frying pan with the wine and a ladleful of warm milk. Cook over a low heat for about 30 minutes, stirring from time to time (more frequently towards the end of the cooking time) and topping up with warm milk as needed until the rice has absorbed the milk and the sauce is thick and creamy.

Stir in the sugar and white chocolate and continue to stir for a few more minutes, adjusting the consistency of the risotto to taste with the boiling water.

Ladle into shallow bowls, decorate with the strawberries and a little grated chocolate and serve with spoonfuls of clotted cream or crème fraîche.

Tip Unfortunately risotto isn't one of those dishes that can be made in advance. However, it could be half cooked before eating the main course then finished off with the remaining milk while you clear the dishes.

Minted chocolate fondants

Although these restaurant-style puddings need to be baked at the very last minute, they can be prepared well in advance and left in the fridge.

Serves 6
Preparation time:
30 minutes + 1–2 hours chilling
Cooking time: 15 minutes

6 tablespoons **double cream**
150 g (5½ oz) **good quality white chocolate, broken into pieces**
1½ tablespoons **chopped fresh mint**
75 g (2¾ oz) **(70% cocoa) dark chocolate, broken into pieces**
75 g (2¾ oz) **butter, plus extra for greasing**
3 teaspoons **cocoa powder**
3 **eggs**
2 **egg yolks**
125 g (4½ oz) **caster sugar**
75 g (2¾ oz) **plain flour, sifted**

To decorate
mint leaves
sifted icing sugar

Bring the cream just to the boil in a small saucepan, add the white chocolate and stir until melted. Cool, stir in the mint and freeze until required.

Put the dark chocolate and butter into a bowl and set over a saucepan of gently simmering water. Leave until melted.

Grease six 150 ml (5 fl oz) ovenproof ramekin or small soufflé dishes with butter then add ½ teaspoon of cocoa to each and tilt the dishes until the insides are coated.

Put the whole eggs, extra egg yolks and sugar in a mixing bowl and whisk for a minute or so until just mixed and frothy. Gradually whisk in the melted dark chocolate and butter. Sift the flour over the top then fold in with a large spoon.

Divide half the chocolate mixture between the dishes (reserve the rest in the bowl) and chill for 1–2 hours to suit you.

When almost ready to serve, preheat the oven to 180°C/350°F/Gas Mark 4.

Take the white chocolate mixture out of the freezer, divide into six then, using two teaspoons, shape each piece into a rough-shaped round. Make a dip in the centre of each fondant, add the white chocolate, then cover with the remaining dark fondant mixture from the reserved bowl.

Bake for 15 minutes on a baking sheet until the tops are slightly domed, the chocolate sponge just set around the edges and the white chocolate centre softened. Serve in the dishes, set on small plates with a few mint leaves and a light dusting of icing sugar, or run a knife around the edges of the dishes, turn the fondants out on to plates and decorate as above. Serve immediately.

Tips If you don't have any fresh mint then leave it out or try adding a little chopped basil or thyme instead. The white chocolate filling can be made the night before and kept in the freezer.

The cooking time is crucial so, as ovens vary, you may find that the first time you make these they are a little too soft or a little too set. If using a fan oven, reduce the temperature by 10–20°C. You are aiming for a lightly set, dark chocolate mousse with a soft, runny white chocolate centre.

Chocolate puddle pudding

As this rather magical pudding cooks, the sponge and sauce miraculously swap places. This is delicious served with vanilla ice cream.

Serves 6
Preparation time:
  30 minutes
Cooking time:
  40–45 minutes

icing sugar, sifted, to decorate

Sponge base
100 g (3½ oz) butter, at room temperature, or soft margarine, plus extra for greasing
100 g (3½ oz) light muscovado sugar
125 g (4½ oz) self-raising flour
25 g (1 oz) cocoa powder
½ teaspoon baking powder
2 eggs
150 ml (5 fl oz) semi-skimmed milk

Chocolate and ginger beer sauce
25 g (1 oz) cocoa powder
100 g (3½ oz) light muscovado sugar
150 ml (5 fl oz) boiling water
300 ml (10 fl oz) ginger beer

Preheat the oven to 180°C/350°F/Gas Mark 4.

Put all the sponge ingredients, except the milk, into a bowl or food processor and beat together until smooth. Gradually mix in the milk. Spoon into the base of a buttered 1.4 litre (2½ pint) pie dish.

To make the sauce, put the cocoa powder and sugar into a bowl, stir in the boiling water until smooth then mix in the ginger beer. Pour the sauce over the top of the sponge so that it is completely covered. Do not be tempted to mix it together.

Stand the dish on a baking sheet and bake in the oven for 40–45 minutes until the sponge is well risen, the top has cracked slightly and the sauce is bubbling around the edges of the dish. If unsure, insert the tip of a teaspoon into the centre of the pudding – the sponge should be a thick set layer on top of the sauce. If it is still slightly soft, cook for another 5 minutes then retest.

Dust the top of the pudding with icing sugar and serve within 10–15 minutes. If the pudding is left to stand the sponge topping will absorb the sauce.

Tip Ginger beer adds a light delicate gingery taste to the finished pudding and can be bought in alcoholic or non-alcoholic versions. However, if serving to young children you may prefer to substitute 300 ml (10 fl oz) of cold water instead.

Chocolate pecan pie

This favourite is made even more heavenly with very dark chocolate. Serve warm with whipped cream flavoured with maple syrup and cinnamon.

Serves 8
Preparation time:
40 minutes + 15 minutes
chilling + 30 minutes
standing
Cooking time: 1 hour

Pastry case

175 g (6 oz) plain flour, plus extra for dusting
50 g (1¾ oz) caster sugar
½ teaspoon ground cinnamon
75 g (2¾ oz) white vegetable shortening or butter, diced

Pecan filling

200 g (7 oz) golden syrup
200 g (7 oz) light muscovado sugar
75 g (2¾ oz) butter, diced
100 g (3½ oz) dark chocolate (70% cocoa), broken into pieces
a pinch of grated nutmeg
¼ teaspoon ground cinnamon
4 eggs
200 g (7 oz) pecan nuts

To make the pastry case, put the flour, sugar and cinnamon in a large bowl. Add the vegetable shortening or butter and rub in with your fingertips or an electric mixer until the mixture looks like fine crumbs. Add 2 tablespoons of water and mix to a smooth dough, adding a little extra water if needed.

Knead lightly then roll out the pastry thinly on a surface lightly dusted with flour.

Butter a 24 cm (9½ inch) round, 2.5 cm (1 inch) deep, loose-bottomed, fluted flan tin. Lift the pastry over a rolling pin and drape into the tin. Carefully press over the base and up the sides then trim the top to about 5 mm (¼ inch) above the top of the tin to allow for shrinkage. Prick the base and chill in the fridge for 15 minutes.

Preheat the oven to 190°C/375°F/Gas Mark 5.

Line the pastry case with greaseproof or non-stick baking paper and baking beans, put on to a baking tray and cook for 10 minutes. Lift the paper and baking beans out and cook the case for 5 more minutes until lightly browned around the edges.

Meanwhile, make the filling by gently heating the syrup, sugar, butter and chocolate in a saucepan, stirring until melted. Take off the heat and cool for 5 minutes then add the spices and gradually beat in the eggs, one at a time, until smooth.

Pour the filling into the pastry case then arrange the pecan nuts on top, either in neat concentric rows or in a random pattern. Cover the top loosely with foil then bake the tart for about 45 minutes until the filling is set and puffed up slightly. Uncover and leave to stand for 30 minutes or until just warm. It will sink level with the top of the pastry case as it cools.

Remove from the tin, transfer to a serving plate, cut into wedges and serve.

Pear and chocolate tart

Buttery pastry encases a rich, moist filling. If you're feeling really decadent, serve with warm brandied chocolate sauce (see page 52).

Serves 6
Preparation time:
 45 minutes + 15 minutes chilling + 20 minutes cooling
Cooking time:
 45–55 minutes

Pastry
175 g (6 oz) plain flour, plus extra for dusting
50 g (1¾ oz) icing sugar
75 g (2¾ oz) butter, diced

Pear and chocolate filling
100 g (3½ oz) butter
100 g (3½ oz) icing sugar
100 g (3½ oz) ground almonds
a few drops of almond essence
2 eggs
100 g (3½ oz) dark chocolate (70% cocoa), melted
3 ripe pears (about 400 g/14 oz)
juice of ½ a lemon
2 tablespoons flaked almonds

To decorate
icing sugar
50 g (1¾ oz) dark chocolate (70% cocoa), diced (optional)

To make the pastry, put the flour, icing sugar and butter into a bowl and rub in the butter with your fingertips or an electric mixer until the mixture looks like fine crumbs. Add 2 tablespoons of water and mix to a smooth dough, adding a little extra water if needed.

Knead lightly then roll out on a lightly floured surface.

Butter a 24 cm (9½ inch) round, 2.5 cm (1 inch) deep, loose-bottomed fluted flan tin. Lift the pastry over a rolling pin and drape into the tin. Carefully press over the base and up the sides and trim the top to about 5 mm (¼ inch) above the top of the tin to allow for shrinkage. Prick the base and chill in the fridge for 15 minutes.

Preheat the oven to 190°C/375°F/Gas Mark 5.

Line the pastry case with greaseproof or non-stick baking paper and baking beans, put on to a baking sheet and cook for 10 minutes. Lift the paper and beans out and cook the tart for 5 more minutes until lightly browned around the edges. Reduce the oven to 180°C/350°F/Gas Mark 4.

To make the filling, beat the butter and icing sugar together until light and fluffy. Add the ground almonds, almond essence and eggs and mix until smooth. Stir in the melted chocolate.

Peel, core and quarter the pears, slice and toss in the lemon juice. Arrange just over half in the base of the tart case. Spoon the almond and chocolate mixture over the top and smooth level. Sprinkle over the remaining pears and flaked almonds.

Bake for 30–40 minutes until the mixture is set, the almonds golden and the pears on the surface are just beginning to brown. (Check after 20 minutes and cover with foil if the flaked almonds appear to be browning too quickly.) Leave to cool slightly for 20 minutes then lift out of the tin and transfer to a serving plate. Dust with icing sugar then sprinkle with extra chocolate if liked – the heat from the tart will soften it slightly. Serve cut into wedges.

Tip This tart freezes well wrapped in cling film or foil. Defrost for 3 hours at room temperature then warm through in the oven.

Steamed fig puddings

A comforting pudding that is ideal after a Sunday roast. If you get delayed, turn the heat down under the steamer and leave for another 15 minutes.

Serves 4
Preparation time:
  20 minutes
Cooking time: 45 minutes

Sponge puddings
100 g (3½ oz) soft margarine or
  butter at room temperature,
  plus extra for greasing
100 g (3½ oz) soft light
  muscovado sugar
2 tablespoons golden syrup
2 eggs
100 g (3½ oz) self-raising flour
25 g (1 oz) cocoa powder
¼ teaspoon baking powder
¼ teaspoon ground mixed spice
100 g (3½ oz) ready-to-eat dried
  figs, finely chopped
8 squares (about 50 g/1¾ oz) dark
  or milk chocolate

Toffee sauce
50 g (1¾ oz) butter
50 g (1¾ oz) light muscovado
  sugar
2 tablespoons golden syrup
150 ml (5 fl oz) double cream

Put all the ingredients for the sponge puddings (except the figs and chocolate) into a bowl and beat with a wooden spoon or electric mixer until smooth. Stir in the chopped figs.

Divide the mixture between four 250 ml (8 fl oz) buttered metal pudding moulds. Press two squares of chocolate into the centre of each mould then smooth the top of the puddings level so that the pudding mixture just covers the chocolate.

Cover the moulds with squares of buttered foil then stand them in the top of a steamer set over a pan of simmering water. Add the lid and steam for 45 minutes or until the tops of the puddings spring back when pressed with a fingertip.

Meanwhile, heat the butter, sugar and syrup for the toffee sauce in a small saucepan, stirring occasionally. When the butter has melted and the sugar dissolved, increase the heat and boil for 2 minutes over a medium heat until just beginning to darken. Take off the heat and stir in the cream. Set aside.

Loosen the edges of the puddings, turn out on to plates with a rim or shallow bowls, reheat the sauce and drizzle around the puddings.

Tip If you have a food processor there is no need to chop the figs first, just put them into the processor bowl with the other pudding ingredients and blitz together.

Last
minute
desserts

Pears with aromatic sauce

Wintery puddings needn't be stodgy. Here, pears are poached in a fragrant blend of spices, then some of the syrup is used to make a delicious sauce.

Serves 6
Preparation time:
  15 minutes + 30 minutes cooling
Cooking time:
  10–15 minutes

300 ml (10 fl oz) **water**
100 g (3½ oz) **caster sugar**
2 **star anise**
5 cm (2 inch) **piece cinnamon stick**, halved
4 **allspice berries**, roughly crushed
2 **pared strips of lemon zest**, removed with a vegetable peeler
1 tablespoon **fresh lemon juice**
6 **Comice or Conference pears**
150 g (5½ oz) **milk chocolate (39% cocoa)**, broken into pieces

Put the water, sugar, spices, lemon zest and juice into a saucepan that will snugly fit the pears and cook over a low heat until the sugar has dissolved.

Peel the pears, leaving the stalks intact, then cut a thin slice off the base so that the pears will stand up when ready to serve. Add to the saucepan, cover and simmer gently for 10–15 minutes, turning the pears once or twice if not fully submerged in the syrup. The timings will vary depending on the size and firmness of the pears. Leave to cool for 30 minutes in the syrup.

Transfer the pears to a serving bowl. Strain and reserve 150 ml (5 fl oz) of the syrup, adding the rest, with the spices to shallow serving dishes. Cut the lemon zest into thin strips and set aside.

Return the measured syrup to the saucepan, bring back to the boil then take off the heat and add the chocolate. Set aside until melted then stir until smooth. Gently warm the syrup again if the chocolate hasn't completely melted but be careful not to let it boil.

Stand the pears in the shallow serving dishes, pour the sauce into a jug and allow diners to pour it over to taste. Decorate with the reserved lemon strips.

Tip Ecuadorian milk chocolate is the best-flavoured chocolate for this sauce as it has a slightly stronger flavour than Swiss milk chocolate. If you can't find it, use either a mix of dark and milk chocolate or all dark chocolate.

Chocolate zabaglione

If you need to rustle up a pudding for unexpected visitors, this is it. Deliciously warm and frothy, serve with crumbled Italian amaretti biscuits.

Serves 4
Preparation time:
  2 minutes
Cooking time:
  5–10 minutes

4 egg yolks
50 g (1¾ oz) caster sugar
25 g (1 oz) cocoa powder (no
  need to sift)
150 ml (5 fl oz) Marsala wine or
  sweet sherry
40 g (1½ oz) amaretti biscuits,
  crumbled

One-third fill a medium saucepan with water and bring to the boil. Put the egg yolks, sugar and cocoa powder into a large mixing bowl and beat with an electric whisk for a few minutes until smooth.

Reduce the heat under the pan to a simmer then set the bowl on top, making sure that the water doesn't touch the base of the bowl. Gradually whisk in the Marsala or sherry and continue to whisk for 5–10 minutes until the mixture is very thick and frothy. Fold in most of the amaretti biscuits. Spoon into dainty glasses and sprinkle with the remaining crumbled biscuits. Serve immediately.

Fruity chocolate sundaes

Need a quick summery pudding? Simmer a can of coconut milk and stir in some chocolate and sugar. Delicious drizzled warm over a fruit salad.

Serves 6
Preparation time:
 10 minutes
Cooking time: 10 minutes

400 ml (14 fl oz) full fat coconut
 milk
100 g (3½ oz) milk chocolate
 (39% cocoa), broken into pieces
1 tablespoon light muscovado
 sugar
2 ripe mangoes
2 bananas
grated zest and juice of 1 lime
12–18 scoops vanilla ice cream
a little grated chocolate or a few
 chocolate curls, to decorate
wafer biscuits, to serve

Pour the coconut milk into a small saucepan and simmer over a medium heat for about 10 minutes, stirring occasionally, until reduced by one-third. Take off the heat, add the chocolate and sugar and stir until the chocolate has melted.

Stand one of the mangoes on its narrowest edge and cut a thick slice off each side to reveal the oval stone. Cut around the stone and reserve the pieces of mango. Make criss-cross cuts in the flesh of each thick slice of mango then press the skin side so that the cubes separate. Cut between the skin and flesh to release the cubes. Cut the skin away from the pieces of mango from around the stone, then dice. Repeat with the second mango.

Slice the bananas, toss in the lime zest and juice then mix with the mango. Layer the fruit and ice cream in six glass tumblers then drizzle a little of the sauce over the top. Pour the rest into a jug. Decorate the sundaes with grated chocolate or curls and serve with wafer biscuits.

Tip Keep an eye on the coconut milk as it simmers as it can easily boil over.

Summer berry fondue

Rather than serving in the traditional way, spoon summer fruits into dishes then drizzle the lusciously creamy white chocolate fondue over the top.

Serves 4
Preparation time:
   10 minutes
Cooking time:
   3–4 minutes

100 g (3½ oz) blueberries
200 g (7 oz) raspberries
200 g (7 oz) strawberries, halved
   or sliced depending on their
   size
100 g (3½ oz) white chocolate,
   broken into pieces
1 tablespoon runny honey
4 tablespoons medium white
   wine
125 ml (4½ fl oz) double cream
a few white chocolate curls, to
   decorate (optional)

Mix the fruits together then spoon into four shallow serving bowls or Champagne glasses.

Put the white chocolate, honey, wine and cream into a small saucepan and heat very gently, stirring occasionally until the chocolate has melted. You could also use a chocolate fondue set, if you have one. Spoon over the fruits and sprinkle with some chocolate curls, if liked. Serve immediately.

Tip For a dark chocolate version, simply swap the white chocolate for dark and add a little caster sugar, in place of the honey, to taste.

Chocolate banana crêpes

These thin, lacy pancakes can be rustled up in next to no time, and the chances are that you will have most of the ingredients already.

Serves 4
Preparation time:
15 minutes + 10 minutes standing
Cooking time: 15 minutes

100 g (3½ oz) plain flour
15 g (½ oz) cocoa powder
1 egg
1 egg yolk
1 tablespoon sunflower oil, plus extra for frying
250 ml (9 fl oz) milk

Ginger custard filling
150 ml (5 fl oz) double cream
135 g individual pot of ready made custard
50 g (1¾ oz) stem ginger in syrup, drained and chopped

To decorate
2 bananas, sliced
icing sugar, sifted
75 g (2¾ oz) dark or milk chocolate, melted

To make the crêpes, sift the flour and cocoa powder into a bowl, add the egg, egg yolk and 1 tablespoon of oil then gradually whisk in the milk until smooth. Leave to stand for 10 minutes.

For the filling, whip the cream until it forms soft swirls then fold in the custard and ginger.

Heat a little oil in a small frying pan, pour off the excess into a cup then add 2–3 tablespoons of the batter and tilt the pan to thinly cover. Cook for a minute or two until the underside is golden.

Loosen with a palette knife then turn or flip the crêpe and cook the second side. Slide out on to a plate and keep hot. Repeat, oiling the pan as needed until all the batter has been used up.

Fold the pancakes into quarters and arrange on plates. Spoon the custard mix in between the folds and add the banana slices. Dust lightly with icing sugar and drizzle with melted chocolate. Serve immediately.

Tip Instead of bananas and ginger, try with some fresh or frozen raspberries and passion fruit. Or, if cherries are in season, lightly cook with a little water and sugar then thicken with cornflour and spoon over the pancakes while still warm.

Chocolate French toast

There are times when you really need a sweet fix. This dessert is great for a Sunday brunch too, maybe followed by an orange and melon salad.

Serves 2
Preparation time:
   5 minutes
Cooking time:
   5–6 minutes

40 g (1½ oz) butter, softened
4 thick slices white or 50/50 white
   and brown bread
50 g (1¾ oz) milk chocolate
   (32% cocoa) or dark chocolate
   (70% cocoa), finely chopped
1 egg
4 tablespoons milk
a few drops of vanilla extract
2 teaspoons sunflower oil
icing sugar, sifted
ground cinnamon (optional)

Spread two-thirds of the softened butter over one side of each of the slices of bread. Sprinkle two slices with the chopped chocolate then sandwich with the remaining bread, buttered side downwards, and press gently together.

Beat the egg, milk and vanilla extract in a large shallow dish, add the sandwiches and turn until evenly coated.

Heat the remaining butter and the oil in a large frying pan. Add the sandwiches, spooning any remaining egg mixture over the top, then fry until the underside is golden. Turn over and cook the second side, pressing the top gently with a fish slice so that the sandwiches stick together as the chocolate melts.

Lift out of the pan, cut into triangles or fingers and dust with sifted icing and a little cinnamon, if liked.

Chocolate cherry tiramisu

This light, fruity version is made by layering coffee-soaked biscuits with mascarpone, white chocolate and cherries from the freezer for speed.

Serves 6
Preparation time:
   15 minutes
Cooking time:
   1–1½ minutes

225 g (8 oz) **frozen red stoned cherries**
6 tablespoons **icing sugar**
250 g (9 oz) **mascarpone cheese**
150 ml (5 fl oz) **double cream**
3 tablespoons **cherry brandy or brandy**
1 teaspoon **instant coffee**
125 ml (4½ fl oz) **boiling water**
100 g (3½ oz) **sponge finger biscuits**
75 g (2¾ oz) **white chocolate, diced**

Microwave the cherries on full power for 1–1½ minutes until defrosted then mix with 2 tablespoons of the icing sugar.

Put the mascarpone cheese and a further 2 tablespoons of icing sugar into a bowl. Gradually whisk in the cream until smooth then stir in the brandy.

Mix the coffee with the boiling water then stir in the remaining icing sugar. Dip half the biscuits into the coffee mixture, one at a time, then crumble into the bases of six glasses.

Spoon half the mascarpone mixture over the biscuits then sprinkle with half the chocolate, half the cherries and most of the cherry juice. Repeat the layers, adding the remaining white chocolate at the very end. Serve within 30 minutes.

Tip Fresh raspberries or sliced strawberries would make a delicious alternative to the cherries.

Hot raspberry trifles

Spoon down through a crisp meringue to the soft marshmallow centre then into custard, fresh raspberries and a wonderfully gooey brownie base.

Serves 4
Preparation time:
   15 minutes
Cooking time:
   12–15 minutes

175 g (6 oz) bought or homemade
   chocolate brownies or
   chocolate sponge
4 tablespoons medium sherry
175 g (6 oz) fresh raspberries
2 x 135 g individual pots ready-
   made custard
2 egg whites
75 g (2¾ oz) caster sugar
50 g (1¾ oz) milk chocolate
   (32% cocoa), coarsely grated

Preheat the oven to 160°C/325°F/Gas Mark 3.

Crumble the brownies or sponge into pieces and divide between four 250 ml (9 fl oz) ovenproof glass dishes. Drizzle the sherry over the top. Divide the raspberries between the dishes then spoon over the custard and level the tops.

Whisk the egg whites until they form stiff, moist-looking peaks then gradually whisk in the sugar a teaspoonful at a time until glossy. Fold in the chocolate then spoon over the dishes and swirl into peaks with the back of the spoon.

Put the dishes on a baking sheet and cook for 12–15 minutes until the peaks of the meringue are golden and the trifles are heated through.

Chestnut chocolate baskets

This easy pudding is perfect to make at the last minute. It is particularly suitable for winter or Christmas entertaining.

Serves 6
Preparation time:
  15 minutes

50 g (1¾ oz) dark chocolate
  (70% cocoa), broken into pieces
150 ml (5 fl oz) double cream
250 g (9 oz) can sweetened
  chestnut spread
2 tablespoons brandy
6 brandy snap baskets
dark chocolate piped decorations
  (see page 9)

Melt the chocolate in a bowl set over a saucepan of gently simmering water.

Meanwhile, whip the cream until it forms soft swirls.

Mix the chestnut spread with the brandy until softened then stir in the melted chocolate. Fold into the cream until partially mixed for a marbled effect.

Spoon the chocolate mixture into the brandy snap baskets. Decorate with piped chocolate decorations.

Tips This creamy chocolate and chestnut mix is also delicious used to sandwich two 20 cm (8 inch) round meringues or pairs of small meringues. If you have some light muscovado sugar then use a mix of half muscovado and half caster sugar in the meringues for a light toffee flavour.

You could also decorate these baskets with dark chocolate curls and a dusting of icing sugar and cocoa powder.

Cakes to impress

Black Forest roulade

The season for fresh cherries is short, so use frozen or drained canned cherries when fresh are unavailable and decorate with chocolate curls.

Serves 8
Preparation time:
40 minutes + several hours cooling + marinating
Cooking time: 15 minutes

225 g (8 oz) dark chocolate (70% cocoa), broken into pieces
5 eggs, separated
175 g (6 oz) caster sugar, plus 3 tablespoons for sprinkling
2 tablespoons hot water
250 g (9 oz) cherries on stalks
2 tablespoons kirsch
300 ml (10 fl oz) double cream
2 tablespoons icing sugar

Preheat the oven to 180°C/350°F/Gas Mark 4. Line a roasting tin with a base measurement of 34 x 23 cm (13 x 9 inches) with a large sheet of non-stick baking paper, snipping into the corners of the paper so that it lines the base and sides of the tin.

Melt 200 g (7 oz) of the chocolate in a bowl set over a saucepan of gently simmering water.

Using an electric whisk, beat the egg whites in a large bowl until they form stiff, moist-looking peaks. Using the still dirty whisk, beat the eggs yolks and sugar in a separate bowl until thick and pale and the mixture leaves a trail when the whisk is lifted above the mixture.

Fold the melted chocolate and hot water into the egg yolks until smooth. Fold in a spoonful of the egg whites to loosen the mixture then gently fold in the remaining egg whites until just mixed.

Pour into the lined tin and tilt to ease the mixture into the corners. Bake for 15 minutes until well risen and the top is crusty. Leave in the tin, cover with a clean tea towel and leave to cool for several hours.

Reserving 8 cherries on stalks for decoration, remove the stalks and stones from the remaining cherries and put into a bowl with the kirsch. Cover and leave to marinate for several hours.

About an hour before serving, pour the cream into a bowl. Add the kirsch from the cherries and the icing sugar. Whisk until the cream forms soft swirls.

Remove the tea towel from the roulade, dip in warm water, wring out and put on the work surface with a narrow edge facing you. Cover with a clean sheet of non-stick baking paper and sprinkle with the 3 tablespoons of caster sugar. Turn the roulade out on to this, remove the tin and peel off the lining paper. Mark a line about 2.5 cm (1 inch) up from the base then spoon over the cream and spread into an even layer. Sprinkle the cherries over the top and roll up the roulade, starting from the bottom edge and using the paper and tea towel to help. Transfer to a serving plate.

Melt the remaining chocolate as before and dip the reserved cherries on stalks into the chocolate until half coated. Arrange on the top of the roulade so that the melted chocolate acts as glue.

Tip This roulade can also be filled with white chocolate ganache (see chocolate flower basket, page 93, for method) using 300 ml (10 fl oz) double cream and 200 g (7 oz) white chocolate and a sprinkling of fresh raspberries and blueberries. Alternatively, spoon whipped cream over the roulade and sprinkle with a little chopped stem ginger and diced fresh mango, or fold some canned, sweetened chestnut purée into some whipped cream with a little brandy for a Christmas roulade.

Irish chocolate cake

This surprising cake is made with Guinness and cocoa powder for a moist, rich flavour that contrasts with the icing and wafer-thin chocolate curls.

Serves 10
Preparation time:
  45 minutes + cooling
Cooking time:
  50–60 minutes

150 g (5½ oz) butter, at room temperature, plus extra for greasing
50 g (1¾ oz) cocoa powder, plus 1 tablespoon for dusting
175 g (6 oz) plain flour
1 teaspoon bicarbonate of soda
½ teaspoon baking powder
250 g (9 oz) caster sugar
3 eggs, beaten
200 ml (7 fl oz) Guinness

Frosting
2 egg whites
100 g (3½ oz) icing sugar
175 g (6 oz) butter, diced, at room temperature
¼ teaspoon vanilla essence
200 g (7 oz) white chocolate curls (see page 8)

Preheat the oven to 160°C/325°F/Gas Mark 3. Butter and dust a 20 cm (8 inch) springform tin with the 1 tablespoon of cocoa powder.

Sift the cocoa powder, flour, bicarbonate of soda and baking powder together into a medium bowl. In a second, larger bowl, cream the remaining butter and sugar together until light and fluffy. Alternately mix in spoonfuls of egg and the flour mixture until all the eggs and flour have been added.

Gradually mix in the Guinness until smooth then pour the cake mixture into the lined tin. Smooth the surface and bake for 50–60 minutes until well risen, the top has slightly cracked and a skewer comes out clean when inserted into the centre of the cake.

Leave to cool in the tin for 10 minutes then loosen the edge, turn out on to a wire rack and peel off the lining paper.

Using a hand-held electric whisk, and in a bowl set over a saucepan of simmering water, whisk the egg whites and icing sugar for about 5 minutes until very thick and glossy. Take the bowl off the heat and whisk for a few more minutes until cool. Gradually whisk in the butter, little by little (don't try to hurry this stage), until all the butter has been added and the frosting is smooth and glossy. Mix in the vanilla essence. If the frosting is too soft to spread, chill for 30 minutes.

Cut the cake into three layers horizontally then sandwich back together with half of the frosting. Spoon a thin layer of frosting over the top and sides of the cake to stick the crumbs in place, then spread the remainder over the cake. Transfer to a serving plate and decorate with the chocolate curls. Store in a cool place until ready to serve.

Tip If the icing begins to split when you add the butter, add 1 tablespoon of hot water and whisk well before adding any extra butter.

Lavender chocolate cake

Made with thick-set lavender honey and lavender flowers, this cake makes a great talking point. For a birthday, add some fine candles and a ribbon.

Serves 8–10
Preparation time:
  30 minutes + 30 minutes firming + cooling
Cooking time:
  40–45 minutes

oil for greasing
50 g (1¾ oz) cocoa powder, plus 1 tablespoon for dusting
175 g (6 oz) plain flour
1½ teaspoons bicarbonate of soda
1½ teaspoons baking powder
1 teaspoon dried or 2 teaspoons fresh lavender petals, plus extra to decorate
50 g (1¾ oz) caster sugar
150 ml (5 fl oz) virgin olive oil
150 ml (5 fl oz) milk
3 eggs
100 g (3½ oz) runny lavender honey
lavender flowers on their stems, to decorate
whipped cream, to serve

Frosting
100 g (3½ oz) thick-set lavender honey
200 g (7 oz) dark chocolate (70% cocoa), broken into pieces
50 g (1 oz) icing sugar
1 tablespoon hot water

Preheat the oven to 160°C/325°F/Gas Mark 3. Lightly oil a 20 cm (8 inch) springform tin, sprinkle over 1 tablespoon of cocoa powder and tilt the tin until the base and sides are well coated.

Sift the remaining cocoa powder, flour, bicarbonate of soda and baking powder into a large bowl then stir in the lavender petals and sugar. Mix the oil, milk and eggs together in a jug.

Add the honey to the flour then gradually whisk in the oil mixture until smooth.

Pour the cake mixture into the tin and level the surface. Bake for 40–45 minutes until well risen and a skewer comes out clean when inserted into the centre of the cake. Leave to cool for 10 minutes, loosen the edge and turn out of the tin on to a wire rack. Leave to cool.

To make the frosting, warm the honey and chocolate in a bowl over a saucepan of barely simmering water, stirring occasionally until the chocolate has melted. Sift the icing sugar and stir into the chocolate with the hot water until the frosting is smooth.

Leave the cake on the wire rack, slide a plate underneath to catch any frosting drips and spoon the frosting over the top and sides of the cake. Smooth with a round bladed knife and swirl the top attractively. Sprinkle the top of the cake with a few extra lavender petals and some flowers still on their stems. Leave for 30 minutes for the frosting to firm up then transfer to a serving plate. Serve cut into slices with whipped cream sprinkled with lavender petals.

Tips Not a fan of lavender? Leave it out and use mixed flower or clover honey, adding a little grated orange zest instead.

If you like, you could cut the cake in half horizontally and use a few spoonfuls of the frosting to sandwich it back together again.

Three-tiered chocolate cake

Spoil milk chocolate fans with this light chocolate cake decorated with pink fondant icing flowers – easily made with plunger cutters.

Serves 40
Preparation time:
  2 hours + cooling + setting
Cooking time:
  20–35 minutes

500 g (1 lb 2 oz) butter, at room temperature
500 g (1 lb 2 oz) caster sugar
9 eggs
625 g (1 lb 6 oz) self-raising flour
75 g (2¾ oz) cocoa powder
4–6 tablespoons milk

Fondant flowers
350 g (12 oz) ready-to-roll white icing
brown and pink or red paste food colourings
cornflour, for dusting

Butter icing
250 g (9 oz) dark chocolate, broken into pieces
250 g (9 oz) butter, at room temperature
500 g (1 lb 2 oz) icing sugar, sifted
2 tablespoons milk

Preheat the oven to 160°C/325°F/Gas Mark 3. Line the bases and sides of a 20 cm (8 inch), a 15 cm (6 inch) and a 7.5 cm (3 inch) deep, round cake tin with non-stick baking paper (see Tip).

Cream the butter and sugar together until smooth. Add the eggs one at a time, alternating with a little flour and mixing in each until smooth.

Add the remaining flour, cocoa powder and enough milk to make a soft dropping consistency. Divide the mixture between the cake tins so they are all a similar height. Smooth the tops.

Bake all the cakes on the centre shelf, allowing about 40–45 minutes for the small cake, about 1 hour for the middle cake and 1 hour 20–35 minutes for the largest one or until a skewer inserted into the centre comes out clean. Leave to cool for 10 minutes then turn out on to a wire rack, peel off the paper and cool completely.

Meanwhile, make the flowers. Divide the icing into four and colour one piece brown and the others varying shades of pink. Wrap each piece of icing separately in cling film so it does not dry out.

Taking a little icing at a time, roll out thinly on a work surface dusted with cornflour. Stamp out flowers with plunger cutters then press into a circle of foam so that the petals curl. Transfer to a tray lined with non-stick baking paper and continue – rolling and stamping until you have a large selection of different sized flowers. Leave to dry and harden for at least 1 hour.

To make the butter icing, melt the chocolate in a bowl set over a saucepan of simmering water. Beat the butter with the sugar until light and fluffy then gradually mix in the chocolate until smooth. Stir in the milk, if needed, to make a soft, spreadable icing.

Trim the cakes so the tops are level then cut each into three layers. Sandwich back together with some of the butter icing.

Put the largest cake on a plate and stack the smaller cakes on top, sticking them in place with a little butter icing and securing them with 2 or 3 long wooden skewers. Spread a little of the butter icing thinly over the tops and sides of the cakes to stick the crumbs in place, then spread most of the remaining icing over more thickly and smooth with a palette knife. Keep a little icing aside for the flowers.

Arrange the flowers over the cake in swathes, right down to the plate, sticking some of the smallest flowers inside the largest ones with tiny dots of butter icing. Leave in a cool place for up to 24 hours or until ready to serve.

Tip To bake the top tier, wash and dry an empty 200 g (7 oz) baked bean or similar can. Remove the top completely then line with non-stick baking paper and put on a baking sheet with the middle sized cake tin.

Strawberry layer cake

This light, whisked sponge is the ideal cake for those that find dark chocolate a little too rich and bitter for their taste.

Serves 8
Preparation time:
   40 minutes + cooling
Cooking time: 10 minutes

4 eggs
100 g (3½ oz) caster sugar
100 g (3½ oz) plain flour
15 g (½ oz) cocoa powder

To decorate
300 ml (10 fl oz) double cream
grated zest of 1 lime
2 tablespoons icing sugar
4 tablespoons chocolate and
   hazelnut spread
400 g (14 oz) small strawberries,
   sliced
100 g (3½ oz) milk chocolate
   (32% cocoa), coarsely grated

Preheat the oven to 200°C/400°F/Gas Mark 4. Line a 33 x 23 cm (13 x 9 inch) Swiss roll tin with a slightly larger piece of non-stick baking paper and snip diagonally into the corners so that the paper lines the base and stands a little above the sides of the tin.

Put the eggs and sugar in a large bowl and whisk with an electric mixer until very thick, pale and mousse-like and the mixture leaves a trail when the whisk is lifted slightly above the mixture.

Sift the flour and cocoa powder over the top then, using a large spoon, gently fold into the whisked eggs in a figure of eight movement. Pour into the prepared tin and tilt the tin to ease the mixture into the corners. Do not spread the mixture or you will knock out the air.

Bake for 10 minutes or until the sponge is well risen and beginning to shrink away from the sides of the tin and the centre springs back when lightly pressed with a fingertip. Leave to cool in the tin.

Lift the sponge and lining paper out of the tin and put on to a chopping board. Trim the outer edge off the two short sides, cut the sponge into three 23 cm (9 inch) long strips and loosen from the paper.

Pour the cream into a bowl, add the lime zest and icing sugar and whisk until it forms soft swirls. Lift one of the sponge strips off the paper and put towards the end of the chopping board. Spread with 2 tablespoons of the chocolate spread then a little of the cream and a thin layer of sliced strawberries, keeping the smaller slices for the very top.

Cover with a second sponge strip and repeat. Add the third sponge strip and press down lightly. Spread the remaining cream thinly over the top and sides of the cake and arrange the remaining strawberry slices in rows over the top. Press the grated chocolate over the sides of the cake with a wide-bladed knife, carefully transfer to a serving plate and keep in the fridge until ready to serve.

Tips If you don't have a Swiss roll tin, measure across the base of the roasting tins that you have and you may find that one of these will be the right size.

If you don't have an electric whisk, put the mixing bowl over a saucepan of gently simmering water and beat with a balloon whisk. The hot water will help to speed up the whisking time but you will still need plenty of elbow grease!

Devil's food cake

A retro favourite made by mixing cocoa to a smooth paste before adding it to the mixture. The cake is filled and coated with a glossy butter icing.

Serves 6
Preparation time:
   40 minutes + cooling
Cooking time:
   50–60 minutes

50 g (1¾ oz) cocoa powder
200 ml (7 fl oz) boiling water
175 g (6 oz) plain flour
¼ teaspoon baking powder
1 teaspoon bicarbonate of soda
100 g (3½ oz) white vegetable
   shortening or butter
250 g (9 oz) caster sugar
2 eggs

Frosting
150 g (5½ oz) dark chocolate
   (70% cocoa), broken into pieces
200 g (7 oz) butter, at room
   temperature
200 g (7 oz) icing sugar
milk and white chocolate curls, to
   decorate (see page 8)

Preheat the oven to 160°C/325°F/Gas Mark 3. Line the base and sides of an 18 cm (7 inch) deep, round cake tin with non-stick baking paper.

Put the cocoa powder in a bowl and gradually mix in the boiling water until smooth. Leave to cool.

Mix the flour with the baking powder and bicarbonate of soda in a small bowl. Cream the shortening or butter with the sugar. Beat in one of the eggs then add a spoonful of the flour and beat until smooth. Add the second egg and gradually beat in the remaining flour then the cocoa paste, mixing well until smooth.

Pour into the lined tin, level the surface and bake for 50–60 minutes until well risen and a skewer comes out clean from the centre. Leave to cool for 10 minutes then transfer to a wire rack and peel away the lining paper.

To make the frosting, melt the chocolate in a bowl set over a saucepan of gently simmering water. Beat the butter and sugar together in a second bowl until smooth then gradually beat in the chocolate until smooth and glossy.

Cut the cake into three layers then sandwich back together with some of the frosting. Spread the remainder over the top and sides of the cake and swirl with a round-bladed knife. Transfer to a flat plate and decorate the top with chocolate curls.

Tip If the frosting is very soft when first spread over the cake, transfer to the fridge for 30 minutes or so to firm up.

See photo on page 5.

Chocolate amaretti torte

Surprisingly, this striking, two-tone sponge casing is not as tricky to create as you may think. The secret is not to overcook the sponge.

Serves 10
Preparation time:
  45 minutes + chilling
Cooking time:
  5–6 minutes

4 eggs, separated
90 g (3¼ oz) caster sugar
2 egg yolks
15 g (½ oz) plain flour
40 g (1½ oz) cornflour
15 g (½ oz) cocoa powder
5 strawberries, halved
cocoa powder, sifted, to decorate
  (optional)

Filling
200 g (7 oz) dark chocolate
  (70% cocoa), broken into pieces
300 g (10½ oz) ready made
  custard
3 tablespoons amaretto liqueur
  or brandy
450 ml (16 fl oz) double cream
75 g (2¾ oz) amaretti biscuits,
  crushed

Preheat the oven to 200°C/400°F/Gas Mark 6. Line three baking sheets with non-stick baking paper, drawing two 20 cm (8 inch) circles on two of the pieces of paper and a 33 x 15 cm (13 x 6 inch) rectangle on the third.

Using an electric mixer, whisk the egg whites until they form stiff, moist-looking peaks then gradually whisk in one-third of the sugar. Using the still dirty whisk, beat all the egg yolks and remaining sugar until thick and mousse-like and the mixture leaves a trail when the whisk is lifted up. Fold in the egg whites, then spoon half the mixture back into the egg white bowl.

Sift the flour and half the cornflour into one of the bowls and gently fold in. Sift the cocoa powder and remaining cornflour over the second bowl and fold in.

Spoon the plain mixture into a large piping bag fitted with a 8 mm (³/₈ inch) plain piping nozzle. Pipe diagonal lines over all the drawn shapes, leaving a nozzle width between each line. Pipe the chocolate mixture into the gaps then bake for 5–6 minutes until the sponge is just cooked and beginning to colour. You may need to cook in two batches.

Quickly invert the rectangle of sponge on to a fresh piece of non-stick baking paper, peel off the lining paper, trim to the size of the original drawn rectangle then cut into two long thin strips. Press the sponge strips around the inside of a 20 cm (8 inch) springform tin, with the lightest side touching the tin.

Trim the sponge circles to a little smaller than the base of the springform tin. Keep the best one for the top and press the other into the base of the tin.

Melt the chocolate in a bowl set over a saucepan of gently simmering water. Take the bowl off the pan and stir in the custard then the liqueur or brandy. Whip the cream until only just beginning to thicken then gradually whisk in the chocolate custard. Stir in the amaretti biscuits then pour into the sponge-lined tin. Add the remaining sponge circle, paler side upwards and press gently down on to the filling.

Chill for 5 hours or overnight, remove from the tin and cut into wedges. Serve with the strawberries. Dust the plate lightly with sifted cocoa, if liked.

Tips This also tastes delicious served with a drizzle of warm dark chocolate sauce.

This dessert can also be frozen (pack into a plastic container for protection). Defrost in the fridge.

Chocolate and coffee cake

This moist dark chocolate cake is made with lightly cooked dates and oil instead of butter and has an almost gingerbread-like texture.

Serves 10
Preparation time:
35 minutes + cooling
Cooking time: 20 minutes

150 ml (5 fl oz) boiling water, plus 6 tablespoons
150 g (5½ oz) dried dates, chopped
50 g (1¾ oz) cocoa powder
3 eggs
150 ml (5 fl oz) sunflower oil
175 g (6 oz) caster sugar
175 g (6 oz) self-raising flour
1½ teaspoons baking powder

To finish
25 g (1 oz) caster sugar
75 g (2¾ oz) pecan nuts
oil for greasing
2 teaspoons instant coffee
1 teaspoon boiling water
75 g (2¾ oz) butter, at room temperature
175 g (6 oz) icing sugar

Preheat the oven to 180°C/350°F/Gas Mark 4. Grease and base line two 20 cm (8 inch) sandwich cake tins with a circle of greaseproof or non-stick baking paper.

Pour the 150 ml (5 fl oz) of boiling water into a saucepan, add the dates, cover and simmer for 5 minutes until softened. Mix the cocoa powder to a smooth paste with the remaining boiling water then leave both to cool.

Put the eggs, oil and sugar into a large bowl and whisk together until smooth. Add the cooled cocoa mixture, flour and baking powder and beat again until smooth. Mix in the dates.

Divide the mixture evenly between the two tins and level the tops. Bake for 20 minutes or until the cakes are well risen and the tops spring back when lightly pressed in the centre with a fingertip. Leave to cool for a few minutes then loosen the edges of the cakes with a round-bladed knife, turn out on to a wire rack, peel off the lining paper and leave to cool.

Meanwhile, add the caster sugar and pecan nuts to a frying pan and heat very gently without stirring until the sugar has completely dissolved. Increase the heat slightly and continue to cook, stirring very gently, until the sugar has turned a pale golden brown and the nuts are evenly coated. Spoon into a single layer on an oiled baking sheet and leave to cool and harden.

Dissolve the coffee in the boiling water. Beat the butter and a little of the icing sugar until soft and smooth then gradually beat in the remaining sugar and coffee until evenly mixed.

Put one of the cakes on a serving plate and spread with half the butter icing. Break the nuts into pieces and sprinkle half on top. Cover with the second cake and spread with the remaining icing and nuts. Cut into wedges to serve.

Tips As an alternative, try sandwiching the cakes with a little chocolate spread and spoonfuls of whipped cream, adding a little extra cream on top and a light dusting of sifted cocoa powder or coarsely grated chocolate.

The cake can be kept in a biscuit tin for 2–3 days but without the caramelised pecans.

Chocolate flower basket

This citrus-flavoured cake is wrapped with a band of white chocolate and topped with frosted flowers, making it a perfect Mother's Day gift.

Serves 10–12
Preparation time: 1 hour +
  chilling + cooling
Cooking time: 1 hour

225 g (8 oz) **butter,** at room
  temperature
225 g (8 oz) **caster sugar**
grated zest of ½ a **lemon**
grated zest of ½ an **orange**
4 **eggs,** beaten
300 g (10½ oz) **self-raising flour**
3 tablespoons **milk**

To decorate
300 ml (10 fl oz) **double cream**
300 g (10½ oz) **white chocolate,**
  broken into pieces
4 tablespoons **blueberry** or
  raspberry jam
100 g (3½ oz) **blueberries**
1 m (40 inches) **fine ribbon**

Frosted flowers
2 tablespoons **caster sugar**
a few **pansy, viola** or **primula**
  flowers in mauve and dark
  blue
1 **egg white**

Preheat the oven to 160°C/325°F/Gas Mark 3. Line the base and sides of a deep 20 cm (8 inch) cake tin with non-stick baking paper.

Cream the butter, sugar and lemon and orange zest together in a large bowl until light and fluffy. Gradually add alternate spoonfuls of beaten egg and flour, mixing well after each addition until smooth. Continue until all the eggs and flour have been added. Stir in the milk to make a soft dropping consistency.

Spoon the cake mixture into the prepared tin and level the surface. Bake for about 1 hour until golden and well risen and a skewer comes out clean when inserted into the centre of the cake. Leave to cool for 10 minutes then turn out on to a wire rack and peel off the lining paper.

Meanwhile, pour half the cream into a saucepan and bring just to the boil. Take off the heat, add 200 g (7 oz) of the chocolate and stir until melted. Leave to cool then chill for 1 hour. Gradually whisk in the remaining cream until thick. Don't be tempted to over whisk or the mixture could separate.

Cut the cake horizontally into three layers. Put the bottom layer on a flat cake plate, spread with half the jam, spoon a little white chocolate cream on top, sprinkle with half the blueberries and repeat with the second cake layer. Add the cake top and spoon the remaining white chocolate cream over the top and sides, making the top a slightly thicker layer.

Melt the remaining white chocolate in a bowl set over a saucepan of gently simmering water. Meanwhile cut a strip of paper that is 65 x 7.5 cm (26 x 3 inches) or the circumference of the cake and just a little taller than the sides. Spoon the chocolate on to the paper so that it covers the paper, forming wavy swirls just under the top long edge.

Carefully wrap the paper around the cake so that the melted chocolate is against the cake and the wavy edge is at the top. Smooth the paper in place, trimming if necessary so that the short edges of the paper just butt together and do not overlap. Chill until firm.

To frost the flowers, brush the egg white over the flower petals then sprinkle with the caster sugar and put on a plate to dry.

When ready to serve, peel the paper away from the side and tie a fine ribbon around the cake. Arrange the flowers on top attractively.

Tip For a special birthday, add some fine coloured candles to the top and decorate with extra blueberries, raspberries and some halved strawberries instead of the flowers.

Beetroot chocolate cake

This might sound like a strange combination but it works incredibly well. The beetroot adds a moistness and depth to the cake that everyone loves.

Serves 10
Preparation time:
  45 minutes + cooling
Cooking time:
  1–1¼ hours

250 g (9 oz) chilled vacuum pack of cooked beetroot in natural juices, drained
250 g (9 oz) butter, at room temperature
250 g (9 oz) caster sugar
4 eggs
250 g (9 oz) self-raising flour
50 g (2 oz) cocoa powder
1 teaspoon vanilla essence

Butter icing
125 g (4½ oz) butter, at room temperature
250 g (9 oz) icing sugar
½ teaspoon vanilla essence
1 tablespoon milk

To decorate
mauve paste food colouring
500 g (1lb 2 oz) ready-to-roll fondant icing
cornflour, for dusting
50 g (1¾ oz) dark chocolate (70% cocoa), melted
1 m (40 inches) x 2.5 cm (1 inch) wide brown ribbon

Preheat the oven to 160°C/325°F/Gas Mark 3. Line the base and sides of a 20 cm (8 inch) deep, round, loose-bottomed cake tin with non-stick baking paper.

Purée the beetroot in a food processor until smooth then scoop out and reserve. Add the butter and sugar to the processor and cream together until light and fluffy.

Gradually mix in the eggs, one at a time, adding a little of the flour after each addition and mixing until smooth before adding the next egg.

Add the remaining flour, cocoa powder and vanilla essence. Mix until smooth then beat in the beetroot purée.

Spoon the mixture into the tin, level the surface and bake for 1–1¼ hours or until well risen, the top is slightly cracked and a skewer comes out clean when inserted into the centre of the cake. (You may need to cover the top of the cake after 45 minutes or so if seems to be browning too quickly.) Leave to cool in the tin for 10 minutes then transfer to a wire rack to cool completely.

To make the icing, beat the butter, half the icing sugar, vanilla essence and milk together until smooth then gradually beat in the remaining sugar. Peel the paper off the cake, cut horizontally into three thin layers then sandwich back together with half the butter icing. Spread the remaining icing thinly over the top and sides of the cake. Transfer to a serving plate.

Knead a little food colouring into the ready-to-roll icing and roll out on a surface lightly dusted with cornflour until you have a circle of about 30 cm (12 inches) in diameter. Lift over the rolling pin, drape over the cake and smooth in place with hands dusted in cornflour. Trim off excess icing and brush away any remaining cornflour from the cake.

Spoon the melted chocolate into a greaseproof paper piping bag, fold the top down securely and snip a tiny amount from the tip with scissors. Mark a circle in the centre of the cake with a 7.5 cm (3 inch) plain biscuit cutter and pipe dots of chocolate on the marked circle (don't pipe them too close together or they will merge together). Pipe swirls and dots of chocolate over the top of the cake. Leave in a cool place for the decoration to set then finish with a ribbon around the sides of the cake. Secure in place with dot of melted chocolate or a pin, but remember to remove the pin just before serving the cake.

Tips If you don't have a food processor, mash the beetroot or roughly chop and purée in small batches in a liquidiser.

For a special occasion, place fine candles just inside the circle in the centre of the cake.

This is also delicious and moist served plain without the buttercream or fondant icing; whipped cream makes a good accompaniment.

Christmas cake

Unusually, this rich fruit cake is flavoured with melted chocolate and glacé ginger for a festive cake with a twist.

Serves 20
**Preparation time: 40
 minutes + 3 hours
 soaking or overnight +
 1 week feeding + cooling**
**Cooking time: 2¾–3¼
 hours**

4 tablespoons brandy, plus
 8 tablespoons to finish
grated zest and juice of 1 lemon
grated zest and juice of 1 orange
2 x 500 g (1 lb 2 oz) bags luxury
 dried fruit
300 g (10½ oz) plain flour
2 tablespoons cocoa powder
1 teaspoon ground cinnamon
1 teaspoon ground allspice
250 g (9 oz) butter, at room
 temperature
250 g (9 oz) light muscovado sugar
5 eggs, beaten
2 tablespoons chopped glacé
 ginger
50 g (1¾ oz) pistachio nuts, left
 whole
100 g (3½ oz) dark chocolate
 (70% cocoa), broken into
 pieces and melted

Put the 4 tablespoons of brandy and lemon and orange zest and juices into a medium saucepan and bring just to the boil. Add the dried fruit and stir together. Cover and leave to soak for 3 hours or overnight, stirring very occasionally.

Preheat the oven to 140°C/275°F/Gas Mark 1. Line the base and sides of a deep 23 cm (9 inch) round cake tin with a double thickness of non-stick baking paper and set aside.

Mix the flour, cocoa powder and spices together. Using an electric mixer, cream the butter and sugar together in a large bowl until light and fluffy then gradually add alternate spoonfuls of beaten egg and flour, mixing between each addition until smooth.

When the eggs and flour mix have all been added, gradually mix in the soaked fruit then the ginger and pistachio nuts. Gradually mix in the melted chocolate.

Spoon the cake mixture into the prepared tin and level the surface. Bake for 2¾–3¼ hours or until a skewer comes out clean when inserted into the centre of the cake.

Leave the cake to cool in the tin then take out and wrap in foil. Feed the cake with 2 tablespoons of brandy every other day for a week. Leave to mature for 3–4 weeks, if time. Decorate as desired.

Chocolate mousse cake

This is an incredibly rich, dark chocolate cake that is ideal for those with a gluten intolerance, but do check that the chocolate is also gluten free.

Serves 8
Preparation time:
   30 minutes + cooling
Cooking time:
   25–30 minutes

250 g (9 oz) dark chocolate (70% cocoa), broken into pieces
100 g (3½ oz) butter, diced, plus extra for greasing
6 cardamom pods
1 tablespoon cocoa powder, plus extra for decorating
5 eggs, separated
150 g (5½ oz) caster sugar
2 teaspoons warm water
crème fraîche, to serve

Apricot compote
200 g (7 oz) ready-to-eat dried apricots, sliced
4 cardamom pods, roughly crushed
2 tablespoons honey
juice of 1 lemon
250 ml (9 fl oz) water

Put the chocolate and butter in a bowl. Crush the cardamom pods with a pestle and mortar, discard the green pods and finely grind the black seeds. Add these to the chocolate and melt over a saucepan of gently simmering water.

Preheat the oven to 180°C/350°F/Gas Mark 4. Butter a 23 cm (9 inch) springform tin, add the cocoa powder and tilt the tin until the base and sides are completely covered. Discard the excess.

Using an electric mixer, whisk the egg whites in a large bowl until they form stiff peaks then gradually whisk in half the sugar, a teaspoonful at a time. Whisk for a minute or two more until thick and glossy. Using the still dirty whisk, whisk the egg yolks and remaining sugar in a second large bowl until thick and pale.

Gradually whisk the melted chocolate and butter mixture into the egg yolks. Fold in the warm water then a large spoonful of the egg whites to loosen the mixture. Gently fold in the remaining egg whites and spoon the mixture into the prepared tin.

Bake for 25–30 minutes until the cake is well risen, the top is crusty and has cracked and the centre is still slightly soft. Leave to cool in the tin – the cake will sink and crack more on cooling.

Meanwhile put all the compote ingredients into a saucepan, cover and heat gently for 5 minutes until softened. Set aside.

When ready to serve, loosen the edge of the cake, remove from the tin and transfer to a serving plate. Cut into wedges, dust lightly with sifted cocoa powder and serve with spoonfuls of crème fraîche and the apricot compote.

Tip Don't have a pestle and mortar? Improvise with the end of a rolling pin and a mug.

Chocolate truffle cake

Finding the perfect cake for the man in your life can be tricky. This mix of extra-dark chocolate cake and boozy truffles could be the answer.

Serves 24
Preparation time:
1½ hours + cooling
Cooking time: 1–1¼ hours

150 g (5 oz) cocoa powder
400 ml (14 fl oz) boiling water
250 g (9 oz) butter
500 g (1 lb 2 oz) light muscovado
    sugar
5 eggs
400 g (14 oz) plain flour
2 teaspoons baking powder

Butter icing

20 g (¾ oz) cocoa powder
2 tablespoons boiling water
150 g (5½ oz) butter, at room
    temperature
300 g (10½ oz) icing sugar
2 tablespoons rum or brandy (to
    match flavouring in truffles)

To decorate

200 g (7 oz) white chocolate
    melted
300 g (11 oz) dark chocolate
    melted
26 small and 16 large Brandy
    truffles (see page 104)

Preheat the oven to 180°C/350°F/Gas Mark 4. Line the base and sides of an 18 cm (7 inch) and a 12 cm (5 inch) deep, square cake tin with non-stick baking paper.

Put the cocoa powder into a bowl and gradually whisk in the boiling water until smooth. Leave to cool.

Cream the butter and sugar together until smooth. Beat the eggs in one at a time, adding a little flour after each egg and beating well until smooth. Gradually mix in the remaining flour, baking powder and cocoa paste and beat well until smooth.

Divide between the cake tins so that both are a similar depth and smooth the tops. Bake for about 45–55 minutes for the small cake and 1–1¼ hours for the larger one or until well risen, the top is crusty and firm but the centre still very slightly soft (test with a skewer). Leave to cool in the tins.

To make the butter icing, mix the cocoa powder with the boiling water until you get a smooth paste then leave to cool. Beat the butter and sugar together until smooth then mix in the cocoa paste and rum or brandy.

Turn the cakes out of the tins, peel off the lining paper and trim the tops level if necessary. Cut each cake into three layers then sandwich back together with some of the butter icing. Spread a little butter icing on top of the larger cake, press the smaller cake on top and secure in place with long wooden skewers. Put on a flat plate or cake board. Spread the remaining butter icing over the tops and sides of the cakes.

Cut four pieces of non-stick baking paper or clear acetate the same size as the sides of the larger cake, and four pieces the same as the sides of the smaller cake. Pipe the white chocolate over the paper or acetate in random squiggles and chill on a baking sheet in the fridge until hard. Spread half the dark chocolate over two small and two large pieces of paper or acetate to create a marbled effect. Press one of the small pieces on to one of the sides of the top cake so that the chocolate is touching the butter icing. Press in place then repeat on the opposite side. Do the same to the lower cake, chill until firm then carefully peel away the paper or acetate. Re-melt the remaining dark chocolate and repeat so that all the sides of the cakes are covered, trimming away any excess paper or acetate so that the sides meet but do not overlap.

Arrange the smaller truffles around the base of the small cake and the larger ones in rows on the very top.

Tips Spread a little dark chocolate on to a piece of non-stick baking paper or acetate, cut into a small rectangle leave to set, then pipe on a name, as if it's a gift card. Chill then peel away the paper and tuck the chocolate among the truffles.

Clear acetate is available from good stationery shops. If you cannot find it, use non-stick baking paper instead.

Coconut meringue cake

This coconut-speckled, macaroon-style meringue is flecked with grated chocolate and finished with cream and pineapple tossed with lime zest.

Serves 8
Preparation time:
  30 minutes + 10 minutes
  standing + cooling
Cooking time:
  25–30 minutes

5 egg whites
¼ teaspoon cream of tartar
225 g (8 oz) caster sugar
1 teaspoon white wine vinegar
75 g (2¾ oz) dark chocolate
  (70% cocoa), coarsely grated
75 g (2¾ oz) unsweetened
  desiccated coconut

To finish
4 slices fresh pineapple, peeled,
  cored and diced
finely grated zest of 1 lime
250 ml (9 fl oz) double cream
coconut curls (optional, see Tip)
25 g (1 oz) dark chocolate
  (70% cocoa), melted

Preheat the oven to 160°C/325°F/Gas Mark 3. Lightly oil two 20 cm (8 inch) sandwich tins and line the bases with a circle of greaseproof or non-stick baking paper.

Whisk the egg whites and cream of tartar together until they form stiff, moist-looking peaks. Gradually whisk in the sugar, a teaspoonful at a time, and continue whisking for a minute or two until the meringue is thick and glossy. Mix in the vinegar.

Fold in the grated chocolate and coconut with a large spoon and divide the meringue between the two prepared tins. Spread evenly then swirl the tops with the back of the spoon.

Bake for 25–30 minutes until the top of the meringue is crisp and very pale golden. Loosen the edges with a round-bladed knife, leave for a couple of minutes then turn out on to a wire rack (the meringues are very fragile, so turn out carefully). Leave to cool.

When almost ready to serve, mix the pineapple and lime zest together. Whip the cream until it forms soft swirls. Peel the lining paper from the meringues then transfer one to a serving plate.

Spoon on just over half the cream and spread to the edges of the cake then add just over half the pineapple. Add the second meringue and decorate with the remaining cream, pineapple and coconut curls, if using. Drizzle with the melted chocolate in random zigzag lines. Leave to stand for 10 minutes then serve.

Tips To make coconut curls, pierce one of the three eyes in the top of the coconut with a skewer or small knife. One of the eyes will be easy, the other two impossible. Tip out the milk into a glass then break the coconut into large pieces by hitting on a very hard surface. Prise the white coconut flesh from the outer shell then pare into thin ribbons with a swivel-bladed vegetable peeler.

For a true taste of the Caribbean, you might like to add a little rum to the whipped cream.

Birthday cake squares

You are never too old to enjoy chocolate birthday cake topped with a rich chocolate and cream cheese frosting and chocolate buttons.

Makes 24 squares
Preparation time:
  30 minutes + firming + cooling
Cooking time: 30 minutes

225 g (8 oz) soft margarine
225 g (8 oz) caster sugar
175 g (6 oz) self-raising flour
50 g (1¾ oz) cocoa powder
1½ teaspoons baking powder
4 eggs

Toppings
100 g (3½ oz) milk chocolate, broken into pieces
200 g (7 oz) cream cheese
300 g (10½ oz) icing sugar, sifted
24 small birthday candles and candle holders
a selection of white and dark chocolate buttons, sweets and sugar sprinkles

Preheat the oven to 180°C/350°F/Gas Mark 4. Line a roasting tin with a base measurement of 18 x 28 cm (7 x 11 inches) with a large piece of non-stick baking paper, snipping into the corners of the paper and pressing it into the roasting tin so that the base and sides are lined.

Put all the cake ingredients into a bowl and beat until smooth (or use a food processor). Spoon the mixture into the tin and level the surface.

Bake for about 30 minutes until well risen and the cake springs back when pressed in the centre with a fingertip. Leave to cool in the tin for 10 minutes then lift the paper and cake out of the tin and cool on a wire rack.

To make the frosting, melt the chocolate in a bowl over a saucepan of gently simmering water. Beat the cream cheese and icing sugar together in a second bowl until just mixed. Spoon half into another bowl then stir in the melted chocolate until smooth.

Peel the paper off the cake and cut in half horizontally. Sandwich it back together with the plain frosting and transfer to a plate or tray. Spoon the chocolate frosting over the top and spread into an even layer. Cut into 24 squares, press a candle holder and candle into the centre of each square then decorate with chocolate buttons, sweets and sprinkles. Leave in a cool place for the frosting to firm up.

Tips The cake can be made and decorated the day before then covered with a dome of foil that is tightly sealed around the base of the plate. Keep in the fridge and allow to come to room temperature before serving.

To make the cake more personal, spoon a little melted chocolate into a greaseproof paper piping bag, snip off the tip then pipe initials of the birthday recipient on to a tray lined with non-stick baking paper. Chill until firm then peel off the paper when needed.

Petits
fours

Brandy truffles

A box of homemade truffles is always well received and needn't be reserved just for Christmas. Why not take to friends instead of a bottle of wine?

Makes 30
Preparation time:
1 hour + 5–6 hours
chilling

150 ml (5 fl oz) double cream
200 g (7 oz) dark chocolate
 (70% cocoa), broken into pieces
2 tablespoons icing sugar
3 tablespoons brandy
cocoa powder, for shaping

To decorate
2 tablespoons cocoa powder
75 g (2¾ oz) white chocolate,
 grated
100 g (3½ oz) dark chocolate
 (70% cocoa), broken into pieces
40 g (1½ oz) milk chocolate
 (32% cocoa), broken into pieces

Bring the cream just to the boil in a small saucepan, take off the heat and add the chocolate. Leave until melted then add the sugar and gradually stir in the brandy until smooth. Leave to cool then transfer to the fridge for 2–3 hours until firm.

Divide the truffle mixture into 30 mounds on a baking sheet then roll into balls with hands dipped in a little cocoa powder.

Put the 2 tablespoons of cocoa powder on one plate and the grated white chocolate on a second. Roll 10 truffles in cocoa powder and another 10 in the white chocolate then arrange in petit four cases. Put these and the undecorated truffles into the fridge for 2 hours until firm.

Melt the dark chocolate in a bowl set over a saucepan of gently simmering water. Take the undecorated truffles from the fridge and rest one on the tines of a fork held over the melted chocolate. Using a teaspoon, spoon over a little of the chocolate until completely covered. Drain off the excess chocolate then put on a piece of non-stick baking paper. Repeat until all the undecorated truffles are coated. Chill for 10 minutes. Melt the milk chocolate, spoon into a greaseproof piping bag, roll the top down then snip off the tip and pipe a decoration on to each chocolate-covered truffle. Return to the fridge until firm once more then transfer to petit four cases. Arrange in a tissue paper-lined box and tie with ribbon.

Tip If you are feeling adventurous, experiment by bringing the cream just to the boil and flavouring with thyme leaves, a few lavender petals or a little chopped chilli. Leave to stand for the flavours to develop then strain and reheat before adding the chocolate. Alternatively, use a gourmet style bar of ready-flavoured chocolate such as chilli, ginger or lime and add these to the hot cream.

Chocolate praline clusters

Choose three or four nuts from a mix of hazelnuts, almonds, cashews, macadamia, pecans, walnuts or pistachio nuts, or perhaps just a single nut.

Makes 12
Preparation time:
  25 minutes + cooling
Cooking time:
  4–5 minutes

oil, for greasing
100 g (3½ oz) granulated sugar
100 g (3½ oz) mixed blanched
  nuts, roughly chopped
1 tablespoon boiling water
15 g (½ oz) butter
100 g (3½ oz) dark chocolate
  (70% cocoa), broken into pieces

Lightly oil a 12-hole mini muffin tin and a small baking tray. Put the sugar, nuts and 5 tablespoons of cold water into a medium-sized frying pan and heat very gently, without stirring, until the sugar has dissolved.

Increase the heat and boil the syrup until it and the nuts have just turned golden. Turn the nuts very occasionally towards the end so that they brown evenly.

Take the pan off the heat and add the boiling water and butter, standing well back and tilting the pan until mixed. When the bubbles have subsided, stir lightly and spoon a little of the praline on to the oiled baking sheet. Divide the rest between the holes in the mini muffin tin and leave to cool.

Melt the chocolate in a bowl set over a saucepan of gently simmering water. Meanwhile, lift the praline off the baking sheet and finely chop.

One at a time, lift the praline clusters out of the mini muffin tin and dip into the chocolate, turning and lifting with a teaspoon and fork. Drain off the excess chocolate and put the clusters on a baking tray lined with non-stick baking paper. Repeat until all the praline clusters have been coated in the chocolate then sprinkle with the finely chopped praline. Leave to set at room temperature or in the fridge then transfer to petit four cases and arrange in a small box then tie with ribbon.

Tips Don't be tempted to stir the praline until the very end or you may crystallise the sugar syrup and spoil the texture of the caramelised sugar.

If you don't have a mini muffin tin, spoon the praline in mounds on to a lightly oiled baking sheet.

Apricot ginger florentines

Dried apricots and cranberries have been added rather than traditional glacé cherries, and the florentines have been flavoured with glacé ginger.

Makes 50
Preparation time:
 45 minutes
Cooking time:
 10–14 minutes

100 g (3½ oz) **butter**
100 g (3½ oz) **caster sugar**
1 tablespoon **golden syrup**
100 g (3½ oz) **ready-to-eat dried apricots**, diced
40 g (1½ oz) **dried cranberries**, chopped
2 tablespoons **glacé ginger** or drained stem ginger, chopped
50 g (1¾ oz) **candied peel**, chopped
100 g (3½ oz) **flaked almonds**

To decorate
100 g (3½ oz) **dark chocolate** (70% cocoa) or milk chocolate (32% cocoa), broken into pieces
100 g (3½ oz) **white chocolate**, broken into pieces

Preheat the oven to 180°C/350°F/Gas Mark 4. Line two baking sheets with non-stick baking paper.

Heat the butter, sugar and syrup in a saucepan until the butter has melted and the sugar dissolved. Stir in the apricots, cranberries, ginger, candied peel and almonds and mix together.

Spoon small mounds of mixture on to the baking sheets and flatten slightly. Bake for 5–7 minutes until the almonds are lightly browned. You will need to do this in batches.

Quickly neaten the edges of the florentines as they come out of the oven by putting a slightly larger plain biscuit cutter over a biscuit. Rotate the cutter to nudge the warm biscuit edges into a neat shape. Repeat with the other biscuits.

Slide the paper and florentines on to a wire rack and leave to cool and harden. Re-line the baking sheets and continue baking in batches until all the florentine mixture has been baked.

Melt the dark or milk chocolate in a bowl set over a saucepan of simmering water. Turn the florentines over, spoon the chocolate over half the biscuits and spread into an even layer. Swirl a fork through the chocolate just before it sets then chill in the fridge until firm. Cover the remainder of the florentines with melted white chocolate in the same way. Pack into a baking paper-lined box to serve.

Tip If not eating on the day of making, store the florentines in a plastic box in the fridge, interleaving the layers with non-stick baking paper.

Chocolate cherry cups

These summery petits fours would add a stylish finish to any smart supper or party table.

Makes 18
Preparation time:
 35 minutes + overnight marinating + 2 hours chilling

18 fresh cherries with stalks
2 tablespoons brandy, cherry brandy or kirsch
100 g (3½ oz) dark chocolate (70% cocoa), broken into pieces
125 ml (4 fl oz) double cream
150 g (5½ oz) white chocolate, broken into pieces

Make a slit in the base of each cherry and remove the stone, leaving the stalk still in place. Put the cherries in a small plastic container, add the brandy or liqueur and leave to marinate overnight.

Melt the dark chocolate in a bowl set over a saucepan of simmering water. Put 18 foil petit four cases into the holes in mini muffin tins, or put cases on a small baking tray if you don't have muffin tins.

Spoon a little chocolate into one of the foil cases then brush over the inside of the case with a fine paintbrush. Repeat until all the insides of the cases have been painted. Chill in the fridge for 10 minutes then go back over each case, brushing any thin areas with any remaining chocolate (re-melt the chocolate if necessary). Chill in the fridge until firm.

Meanwhile, bring the cream just to the boil in a small saucepan, add the white chocolate and stir until melted. Chill for 1 hour.

Gradually whisk the brandy or liqueur from the marinated cherries into the chocolate cream until it forms soft swirls, being careful not to over whip. Spoon into a piping bag fitted with a small star nozzle.

Lift the foil cases out of the muffin tins, pipe the white chocolate cream into the cases then top each with a cherry. Chill until ready to serve.

Tip If making these when cherries are out of season, use well-drained canned cherries instead and put these underneath the piped white chocolate cream.

Chocolate thins

These must be the easiest petits fours to make. They look particularly attractive if different batches are made with white, milk and dark chocolate.

Makes 30
Preparation time:
   10 minutes + 1 hour chilling

100 g (3½ oz) dark chocolate (70% cocoa), broken into pieces
1 tablespoon runny honey
grated zest of ½ a small orange and 1 tablespoon orange juice
grated zest of ½ a lime and 2 teaspoons lime juice
75 g (2¾ oz) fruit and nut selection, roughly chopped (see Tip)
1 tablespoon pumpkin seeds, roughly chopped

Melt the chocolate and honey in a bowl set over a saucepan of gently simmering water. Stir in the orange and lime zest and juice until smooth and glossy.

Drop well-spaced, heaped teaspoonfuls of the mixture on to a baking sheet lined with non-stick baking paper. Spread each into a round about 4 cm (1½ inches) wide with the back of the spoon.

Sprinkle with the chopped fruit and nut mixture and pumpkin seeds then chill in the fridge until firm. Peel off the paper and pack into a small box lined with a clean square of non-stick baking paper. Add a lid and tie with ribbon.

Tip Fruit and nut selection is a gourmet-style blend that often includes whole cashews, unblanched almonds, pecans, pistachio nuts, dried cranberries, raisins and sultanas. It is sold in packs alongside the other nuts and seeds in the supermarket and is a cheap way of using a wide selection of fruit and nuts in a small quantity. You could also use a breakfast cereal topper or make up your own mix, depending on what you have in your cupboard.

Peppermint creams

These are fun to make with young children. Choose different shaped cutters, making sure that they are bite-sized, and have fun with the colours.

Makes 80
Preparation time:
25 minutes + 2–3 hours drying

1 tablespoon liquid glucose
1 egg white or dried egg white powder reconstituted with water
a few drops of peppermint essence
500 g (1 lb 2 oz) icing sugar, sifted, plus extra for dusting
pink and mauve edible paste colouring
100 g (3½ oz) dark chocolate (70% cocoa), broken into pieces

Put the liquid glucose, egg white and a little peppermint essence into a bowl or food processor and gradually mix in enough icing sugar to make a ball. If not using a processor, start with a wooden spoon and then squeeze the mixture with your hands when it becomes too stiff to mix. You may not need all the sugar.

Knead until smooth on a work surface dusted with a little icing sugar. Cut the dough in half. Knead a little pink colouring into one half and a little mauve into the other half so that the food colourings make a marbled effect.

Roll out the pink icing thinly then cut out heart shapes or circles with tiny biscuit cutters. Reroll the trimmings and continue until it is all used up. Repeat with the mauve icing.

Leave the peppermint creams to dry on baking sheets lined with non-stick baking paper for at least 2 hours.

Melt the dark chocolate in a bowl set over gently simmering water. Dip the peppermint creams, one at a time, into the chocolate until they are half covered then leave to dry on the paper-lined trays. Pack into small boxes to serve.

Index